W9-DDJ-177

Bad Dogs Have More Fun

SELECTED WRITINGS
on Family, Animals, and Life

by John Grogan
for *The Philadelphia Inquirer*

MJF BOOKS
New York

Published by MJF Books
Fine Communications
322 Eighth Avenue
New York, NY 10001

Bad Dogs Have More Fun
LC Control Number: 2011932134
ISBN-13: 978-1-60671-074-6
ISBN-10: 1-60671-074-5

This edition is published by MJF Books in arrangement with
Vanguard Press, a Member of the Perseus Books Group.

Printed in the United States of America

QF   10   9   8   7   6   5   4   3   2   1

Contents

PART ONE

⌐Family

Deaf Girl Provides Lesson in Courage   3

Food for Thought on Child-Rearing   5

Phila. in Spring, and Free Parking!   8

A Refresher Course in Parenting 101   10

Girl, 4, Offers Hope by Way She Lived   13

A Friendship Born of Two Mothers' Grief   15

A Wish: One More Magic Christmas   17

For Teen Mother, the Son Is Rising   20

Mother Keeps the Passion Alive   22

Getaway Becomes Dad-Son Mind Trip   24

Brain-Damaged, but Still a "Gift"   27

Speeder Dad Learns an Important Lesson   29

Introducing a Gift Named Danny   32

When a Child Goes Missing   34

"It's Never the Same": Too True   37

Who's a Father? A Guy Who's There   39

Learn the Rhythm of Solitude   41

PART TWO

Animals

What's Good for the Goose? Us   47

A Feline Air Traveler Lost in Philadelphia   49

Saying Farewell to a Faithful Pal   52

They're Bad, and We Love 'Em Still   54

Shelter in Media Mocks Its Mission   57

Animal Lovers? No, Just Bullies   59

In the Next Ring, a Stepford Terrier   61

Marley & Me: The Whole Truth   64

Zoo Hysteria High as Elephant's Eye   66

Puppy Mills Not Always Obvious   68

Celebrity & Me   71

A Trek to the North Pole, for His One True Friend   77

Alpha Bet   79

Skip the Gun, Try Four-Legged Security   82

PART THREE

Life

New Scribe: A Suburbanite Geek   87

Spreading Cheer the Interfaith Way   89

Weather to Croon and Swoon Over   92

Boob Eyes Tube While Driving   94

Ditch the Speedo, and Other Fla. Tips   97

9/11 Altered Our View of Tragedy   99

Her Shop Corners Market on Dignity   101

Taking a Shot at Buying a Gun   104

Tired of Sales Calls? Try Defense Tactics   106

Burning the Flag as an Act of Love   109

In Healing, Reminder of Life's Final Hurt   111

Phones Driving Us to Distraction   114

Hey, Ever Hear of an Ashtray?   116

Letting Go of the One That Got Away   119

Haunting Glimpse at a Stranger's Life   121

Let No Chip Put This Vow Asunder   124

He Helps Iraq's Children and America's Cause   126

TV Weather Is a Flurry of Hysteria   129

Ordinary People Vowing to Marry   131

Sounds of Spring Roar in the Burbs   133

Earth Versus the Mall People   136

Tow-Truck Driver Became Her Angel   138

James Pratt: A Knight in a Lime-Green Tow Truck   141

Zero Tolerance Running Amok   143

It's Unhealthy, but It Is Legal   145

The Nonsense Logic of Angry Smokers   148

A Shared Concern for a Jane Doe   150

A Friend Lost in Life, but Found in Death   153

Honked Off by Bumper Sticker   155

When Our Fears Lead to Prejudices   157

A Terrorist? Moi? Twice Exonerated   160

Even Vicki Needs to Work on Image   162

When Music Died, Words Were Born   164

You've Got Spam: AOL's Trial CDs   167

With This Ring, Show Some Class   169

A Helping Hand, a Helping of Grace   172

Summer and Smoke   174

One Violent Summer, Two Worlds Collided   177

Talkin' 'Bout the Generations   180

Dogged Writers in the Big House   182

A Searing Lesson in Forgiveness   185

Flying's Fearful New Annoyances   187

Mortality Check Is in the Mail   190

Just Say No to Black Friday   192

An Army of One Takes on Litter   195

Family

Deaf Girl Provides Lesson in Courage

aitlin Reel was just six months old when her mother knew something
is wrong.

The baby did not respond to voices or sounds, not even a loud clap of
e hands. The doctors told Luann Reel not to worry. Her baby was fine.

But the mother persisted, and when doctors finally tested Caitlin's
aring a year later, they confirmed her fears.

Caitlin was living in a world of silence. She was profoundly deaf.

Flash forward ten years to last week at Shady Grove Elementary School
Ambler. The gymnasium was filled for the winter concert.

Music teacher Ryan Dankanich stepped to the microphone and told
e audience they were about to hear "a very special violinist." The only
ie he gave that this student had made a particularly arduous journey
re was when he said, "Make sure you applaud very loudly."

And then out walked Caitlin, now 11, the deaf baby who never learned
give up. She lifted her violin to her chin and took a deep breath.

In the audience, Luann, the proud mom, stood poised with a video
nera. Her hands were shaking.

"I was really worried," she said later from the family's home in Park-
e in Delaware County. "She had crossed a lot of barriers to get here. I
In't want something really unpleasant to come out of her violin."

3

A Long, Hard Battle

What a long road it had been. From birth, her daughter had been misunderstood, stared at, whispered about, incorrectly labeled—even by teacher—as mentally retarded.

Caitlin set out to prove them wrong. She learned sign language and t rudiments of speech. She received a cochlear implant, which allows her hear some sound. A major accomplishment came last fall when she dered a Big Mac and fries all on her own.

While her hearing brother, Jared, 9, walks two blocks to school, Cait must ride 45 minutes or more each way. The Perm Delco School Distr buses her to Shady Grove Elementary, which has a program for hearir impaired students run by the Montgomery County Intermediate Unit.

Caitlin saw hearing students arriving with musical instruments and s she wanted to play, too. And so, despite all odds, she began violin lessons the first deaf child at the school to attempt them.

"It's taken a tremendous amount of concentration and perseverance her part to get to this point," said Melanie Stefanatos, Caitlin's hearir support teacher.

And last week's concert was her chance to show the world.

The audience hushed. Caitlin drew the bow across the strings. And came . . . music. Slow, sweet, and steady—and with rock-solid timing. S played "Mary Had a Little Lamb" and "Twinkle, Twinkle Little Star."

Her mother fought back tears.

"I know she's not playing Tchaikovsky," Luann Reel, who is divorc said. "But this is my deaf daughter—and she's playing the violin."

An Incredible Feat

For most children, the brief performance would be just one of many K dak moments on the road to adulthood. For Caitlin, it was a Hercule leap. To play this handful of notes, she had to overcome more obstac than most of us will face in a lifetime.

As Dankanich, the music teacher, put it: "It's just an incredible feat she's een able to accomplish."

Caitlin probably will not go on to become a famous musician. She oesn't need to. The violin already has taught her about courage and per-everance and faith.

A girl without hearing tackled an instrument that has everything to do ith hearing, and she didn't give up. For the determined, she learned, ven the steepest mountains can be scaled, one step at a time.

Her performance over, Caitlin hurried off the stage. Principal Beth earson told the 500-member audience the truth about Caitlin—that she as one of the school's seven deaf children.

The audience roared its approval—loudly enough, in fact, that Caitlin uld hear the clapping through her cochlear implant.

Backstage she signed to her mother: "I'm so happy. They were clapping r me. They were clapping for me."

April 14, 2003

Food for Thought on Child-Rearing

he book arrived unannounced in plain brown paper.

On the cover was a photograph of a little girl beneath the title, *Too luch of a Good Thing: Raising Children of Character in an Indulgent ge.*

Hmmm. Was someone trying to tell me something?

A note inside solved the mystery. It was from an old high school friend ho had done well enough financially to retire from his career as an in-stment adviser at the ripe old age of 45.

The way my investments have been going, I'll be working until I'm 95. ther than that, we have a lot in common.

We each have two boys and a girl of similar ages. We each live in nice burbs with good schools where most children grow up assuming a

God-given right to a minimum of 3,000 square feet of air-conditione
living space.

We each worry about what effect all this comfort will have on o
children. Nothing instills more dread in either of us than the S wor
Spoiled.

And so he sent me the book with the caveat, "not that you need this
Like heck I didn't. My idea of tough love is saying no three times befo
caving in.

The book, by Harvard psychology professor Dan Kindlon, has bee
around for a couple of years and covers the obvious bases: the perils
focusing on career over children, on wealth over relationships, on indu
gence instead of consequences.

Or as Kindlon put it, "Giving too much and expecting too little."

Breaking Bread

The book is filled with anecdotes of parents doing all the wrong thin
to win their children's love—including hiring lawyers to help the
avoid the consequences of their bad actions. (Remember the student
Philadelphia's Chestnut Hill Academy last fall whose parents hired
lawyer to beat a deserved expulsion for secretly videotaping a fema
student?)

What makes this book different from the other parenting claptr
out there is its solid research. One fact jumped out at me—th
quantifiable correlation between family meals and children who a
blessedly normal.

Kindlon's research and a number of other national studies reach th
same conclusion: Families that eat most meals together—and that mea
with Dad at the table—have children who are at a significantly lower ri
for drug abuse, depression, promiscuity, and underachievement.

Easy enough. But I had to admit that work hours and long commut
had lately conspired to keep me away from the dinner table more tim
than not.

Last week, I found Kindlon at home in Boston during a break in a
blicity tour for his new book, *Tough Times, Strong Children*, and
pped the question: Is it really that simple?

In a word, yes. Sitting down as a family, even if it is microwaved pizza, is a
y to reconnect, share, and bond, Kindlon said. It lends structure and pre-
tability and balances the negative influences of popular culture and
ong-track friends.

Hey, and you get to eat! I'm in.

Fighting Back

asically, kids don't get in trouble as much when they are alone as when
y are with friends," he said. "So when you allow the peer group to
ve more influence than the family, you're increasing your child's risk.
ose family dinners are a time to remind the child: This is what we be-
ve in, this is our view of the world."

But why dinner? Wouldn't, say, family walks do the same thing? Per-
s, but Kindlon suspects the food itself has a healing effect.

"Feeding kids, nurturing them—it's what parents do," the professor
l. "There's something almost primordial about parents supplying food
heir kids that cements the bond."

I also spoke with William Lessa, superintendent Hatboro-Horsham
ool District, who will speak tomorrow night at the Parenting Center
Abington on the importance of fathers.

Lessa agrees family meals are key.

"In our family, dinner was pretty much sacred," the father of two said.
ids clearly need food. They also need guidance; they need structure;
y need love." All of which can be provided around the dinner table.

So bring on the lasagna. Tonight, I swear, I'm wrapping up early and
ng down where I belong—at dinner with my family.

April 21, 200

Phila. in Spring, and Free Parking!

Some vacations just aren't meant to be. Our long-anticipated fami
spring break was one of them.

The plan was to drive to Williamsburg, Virginia, for five days of t
kind of family togetherness you can achieve only by cramming fi
people into a standard hotel room. We would see the historic sites, eat
colonial taverns, buy tacky souvenirs, and swim at the hotel's indoor po

That was the plan.

A friendly little stomach bug known as rotavirus had other ideas. Fi
it laid out my older son, then my daughter. Then my wife. Hey, gar
How's the vacation going so far?

According to the Centers for Disease Control and Prevention, r
tavirus kills 600,000 children worldwide per year, mostly from deh
dration brought on by relentless vomiting and diarrhea. In the Unit
States, it lands 55,000 children in the hospital every year to recei
intravenous fluids.

Two of them were my kids. It wasn't Busch Gardens, but the hospi
did hand out free Easter baskets.

We stayed in denial for as long as possible, canceling our hotel reser
tions one night at a time.

By the weekend, with the patients resting comfortably in the Grog
Ebola Ward, my one remaining healthy child and I decided to salva
what little scrap of our derailed vacation we could. "Grab a jacket," I sa
"We're going to Philadelphia."

Been There, Done That

"You're not dragging me to the Liberty Bell again, are you?" my ni
year-old asked suspiciously. I shook my head no.

"Promise?"

"Promise."

And so we were off—with apples, water bottles, and bicycles.

By 10 a.m., we were parked off Kelly Drive. The day was as flawless as
ril days get, the air crisp, the cherry and pear trees in glorious bloom.

In Fairmount Park, we counted hawks and climbed rocks. Along the
uylkill, we hung our feet over the water and waved to the rowing
ms.

We pedaled north along the east bank of the river and then south
in. You think driving on Interstate 95 is a death trap? Try the Kelly
ive bike path on a beautiful spring Sunday.

The whole city, it seemed, was on this path, enjoying the morning. We
dged speeding rollerbladers (an alarming number of them skating—this
ot a misprint—backwards), strolling couples, darting toddlers, prancing
s, and zipping cyclists.

Mostly, though, we dodged breathtakingly athletic, beautifully chiseled
ners of every hue, every one of them with great teeth. To them I'd just
to say thanks for making me feel only slightly older than King Tut.

Eventually, we made our way to the Philadelphia Museum of Art,
ere a band was playing near the front steps.

"C'mon," I said, "Let's run up the stairs, just like in the movie."

"Uh, what movie?"

Oy. Kids nowadays—no culture.

Up and Away

ran up, anyway, me singing the *Rocky* theme song (now there's some-
g no one's ever thought to try before), my son singing the "I've Got
Doofus Dad Humiliation Blues."

From the top, we gazed out over the urban skyline, this City of Broth-
Love newly dear to our hearts. I yelled the first thing that came to
d: "Hey! Come back with our bikes!"

Just kidding. The bikes, unchained and unattended, survived u
touched.

We sat on the sidewalk and ate semi-petrified hot dogs that I'
pretty sure had been spinning on the rotisserie since before the Riz
administration.

"Dad, these are the best hot dogs I've ever had!" the kid raved.

We stuck our heads inside dinosaur jaws at the Academy of Natu
Sciences, marveled at the bathroom habits of the horses waiting to gi
carriage rides in the historic district, and traipsed through the Betsy R
house, where it was all Dad could do not to crawl into the Widow Lit
gow's bed and catch a few winks.

Best of all, we managed to nab free parking right on Arch Street. "So
I said solemnly, "I want you to stop and reflect on this moment. It w
likely never be repeated in your lifetime."

And so went our Philadelphia mini vacation. We came; we ate b
food; we avoided personal collisions—and no one got sick. All in all, no
bad way to spend a lovely spring day.

June 10, 20

A Refresher Course in Parenting 101

Good morning, class, and welcome to Parenting 101.

The purpose of this refresher course is to reinforce some of the ba
skills we parents need to raise stable children who will grow up to
something other than residents of one of our fine local penitentiaries.

I apologize in advance if some of these points seem frightfully obvio
But a spate of parenting no-nos in recent months has shown that, whe
comes to rearing children, it's best not to take anything for granted.

For instance, when in doubt, do not—I repeat, do not—punch
your son's Little League coach. I know all the other parents are doing
but just keep telling yourself, "I am the role model. I am the role mod

Vhen your 14-year-old has her classmates over for a sleepover, the
per question is not: "Do you kids take your margaritas with salt?"

oday's course uses actual news events from around our region to illus-
helpful parenting dos and don'ts. So let's get started.

eal news items: A 29-year-old woman was found guilty of leaving her
onth-old son in the car while she shopped at a J.C. Penney store in
theast Philadelphia. In Evesham, a 31-year-old woman was charged
leaving her two young children in a car for more than an hour while
was at a job interview.

arenting 101 tip: Until Ford releases the Nannygate SUV, we suggest
take advantage of a little-known service available to parents in which
ed individuals will actually come to your house and watch your chil-
for a modest hourly fee. It's called baby-sitting.

eal news item: A father and his 19-year-old son were arrested in West
ster after a chase and charged with a string of home burglaries.

arenting 101 tip: When we stressed the need for father-son bonding
ortunities, we more had in mind touch football and weekend fishing
.

eal news items: A Southwest Philadelphia woman was charged with
ng duct tape over her 7-month-old son's mouth because he was
ag too much. In a separate case, a Bucks County woman was charged
wrapping two foster children and a biological child in duct tape,
her estranged husband was charged with photographing the bound
dren.

arenting 101 tip: Yes, it's true that children need certain constraints in
lives. And it's true that duct tape has many useful purposes around
ouse. But let's keep those two thoughts separate.

eal news items: Police said a 7-year-old girl steered the family auto
n the Blue Route last year at speeds ranging from 5 to 50 mph, while
drunken mother worked the brake and gas pedals.

arenting 101 tip: When we said "designated driver," we were thinking
meone old enough to see over the dashboard. Ever hear of a taxi, lady?

Real news item: Ebony Smith, 10, of Philadelphia, was released f
the hospital last month after she was shot in the head in February foll
ing a snowball fight. Arrested in the drive-by shooting was the moth
another girl who was hit by a snowball, and the woman's fiancé.

Parenting 101 tip: I'm not sure what's scarier, the right to bear arn
the right to bear children. Put them together and you have a good a
ment for licensing both.

Real news item: A Fort Washington woman is awaiting trial on ch
that she embezzled $65,000 from the Horsham Hawks during her te
as the youth football league's treasurer. Her husband was convicte
slugging another parent, the Hawks' president, in the nose during a
frontation about the missing money.

Parenting 101 tip: While we laud the spirit of volunteerism, in this
we must point out that draining the college fund is a more efficient
of stealing from your children. And, dads, Mike Tyson is probably no
best model for resolving disputes.

Finally, we here at Parenting 101 have received several repor
parents buying alcohol, condoms, and motel rooms for their unde
children.

(All in good fun, right?)

Mom and Dad, we know you want to be the coolest parents ir
PTA. But sometimes a grown-up just has to say no. Bummer, huh?

Now get out there and give it a try.

Class dismissed.

August 29, 2003

Girl, 4, Offers Hope by Way She Lived

Our Lady of Mount Carmel Church in Doylestown yesterday, a small ite casket sat at the edge of the altar, its lid opened to show the frail dy of a young fighter.

Her name was Katie Ann Duffin, and she would have turned 5 this ek. Instead, about 300 people gathered on a lovely summer's day to say odbye to this little girl who faced down cancer with a bravery and timism seldom seen in anyone of any age.

All morning long, the people came. They filed past in a long, slow pro- sion, each one greeted with a hug from Katie's parents, Paul and Terry ffin of Doylestown. Many who came had known the girl. Others had ver met her but felt they somehow knew her, too.

It was because of her Web site, www.katieduffin.com, which faithfully onicled in weekly journal entries her long battle against what she led the blob growing inside her.

The Web site was written in her voice by her uncle, Hugh Saunders, to ture her fighting spirit. It started as a way to keep friends abreast of her dical progress, but it grew into something bigger. From across the intry, countless strangers logged on to follow her struggle to survive, ny of them leaving her messages of support in her online guest book.

Her story begins six months after her birth on August 23, 1998, en doctors discovered a golf-ball-size malignancy beneath her left oulder. They operated twice and subjected her to six rounds of emotherapy. As Katie's journal states, "All was great until four years er, almost to the day."

In March, the blob returned. And this time it had long tentacles that ched up along her spine. And that's where Katie's weekly entries begin:

March 11: "The doctors told us that the golf-ball thing is back again

near my shoulder and neck. . . . They decided that they would have t
operations, one from the back and one from the front."

March 22: "I am feeling OK and even asked my mom if I could go
school yesterday. It took a little convincing but she let me go. I had a gr
time. I am not going to let this thing slow me down."

April 6: "Tomorrow is the big day. The doctors will be giving me t
'funny juice' again to make me go to sleep so they can go in and get
rest of the golf ball out of my shoulder."

April 7: "Great news! . . . Dr. Greg just came in and told my mom a
dad that the [spinal] fluid is clear—no bad cells in my spine. I think t
time mom and dad were crying because they were happy, and that ma
me happy."

And so the entries go, swaying from the dire to the mundane, throu
surgeries and radiation treatments and chemotherapy and nausea a
morphine drips. And always there is Katie's voice, the voice of a li
fighter unwilling to throw in the towel.

May 23: "I told [the doctor] he is not dealing with the ordinary
tient. I am Katie Duffin, a mean lean fighting machine."

But by early July, Katie was unable to keep food down and was put
a feeding tube. She was dogged by constant headaches. And in mid-J
came very bad news: The malignancy had spread to her brain. "OK, gu
now is the time to really rally the troops and give me as many prayer
you can muster," one entry states.

July 21, the final entry written in her voice: "I am definitely hanging
there."

The last entry, signed by her parents and older brother, Paul Jr., v
logged August 12: "Hello everyone. This is the update that we knew v
coming but we never wanted to write. Today at 9:30 p.m., Katie finally
lowed the angel to take her hand and show her the way to heaven."

At yesterday's Funeral Mass, the Rev. Charles Hagan noted that this
markable girl's short life "touched so many thousands of people," many
them through her Web site. And to each she offered a message.

'She never, ever, ever gave up hope," the priest said. "This is her legacy
ıs."

~~~~~~~~~~⊃ *September 19, 2003*

A Friendship Born of Two Mothers' Grief

eline: SHANKSVILLE, Pennsylvania.

ıs I stood last week overlooking the hillside near this tiny western
ınsylvania farm town where Flight 93 crashed two years ago, I was
vn to a sun-bleached photograph.

t hung from one of the 40 painted angels planted here to memorialize
ı of the passengers and crew who died that day. The photo shows an
ıctive woman with lustrous dark hair, bright eyes, and a carefree smile.

Ier name was Honor Elizabeth Wainio. She was 27, a rising regional
ıager for Discovery Channel stores in Watchung, New Jersey. And she
 been on her way to a business meeting in San Francisco when her life
ed in this field at 10:06 a.m. on September 11, 2001.

ıs I contemplated this young life cut short, an older woman stepped
ınd placed a red rose beneath the photo. She stood there a long time.
Vhen the woman turned to leave, I asked, "Did you know her?"

he thought for a moment, then said: "Not exactly. Not while she was
ː."

ınd thus began one of the countless untold stories that continue to
 from the ashes of the 9/11 tragedy.

t is the story of two mothers from very different worlds—one a rural
·istian farm wife, the other an urban Jewish professional—finding
ce and dear friendship in shared grief.

A Snowstorm and Death

· woman with the rose, I learned, is Shirley Hillegass, a grandmother who lives with her husband, Robert, on 245 verdant acres of corn and about three miles from the crash site.

During a treacherous snowstorm in 1994, her daughter, Annette, was killed in a car crash.

Hillegass thought she had boxed up her sorrow as much as a mot could. "You don't ever get over the loss," she said. "You just learn to cept the fact that this is the way it is; this is the way it will always be."

Then came the terrorist attacks, and she found the wound wide o again. One victim in particular touched her. It was Elizabeth Wainio, young woman in the photograph.

She seemed like Annette in so many ways. Both were vivacious, an tious, so full of life.

Six months after the attack, at a memorial service in Shanksville which virtually the whole town turned out, Hillegass, as chance wo have it, found herself sitting behind Wainio's stepmother, Esther H mann, a one-time banker from Baltimore.

"I can't explain it. I'm normally not someone to speak to a strang Hillegass said. "I just did what my heart told me I had to do. I don't kn if it was an angel or Annette saying, 'Mom, you need to reach out to woman.'"

So, after the service, she summoned her nerve and introduced herse

"I Love You, Mom"

Heymann, who married Wainio's father when the girl was 5 and lo her as her own, was who Wainio called by Airfone in the minutes be the doomed plane crashed. She was the one to hear her stepdaughter' nal words: "They're getting ready to break into the cockpit. I have to g love you, Mom. Good-bye."

In the months that followed, those words hung like unbearable wei around Heymann's neck. Into that all-consuming grief stepped anot mother, a self-described "country hick," who understood it first-hand.

Heymann said she was leery of strangers trying to befriend her a

e crash. But Hillegass was somehow different. "I had an instinct about
s woman's genuineness," she said. "I just knew she was very special."

The friendship began cautiously with a few respectful words followed
letters and phone calls. Over the months, the women have bonded like
ters. A week ago today, the day after the second anniversary of that aw-
l morning, they met at Hillegass's farmhouse near the crash site to hug,
change small gifts, and simply talk.

"I don't know if I literally believe in angels, but I know there are a lot
people walking around on earth who are angels," Heymann said. "And
irley is one of them."

For her part, Hillegass said the healing has been mutual. "She's helped
e as much as I've helped her," she said.

Two daughters. Two deaths. Two mothers bonded in grief. And, slowly,
gether, a dawning realization that for the living, life goes on.

⌐⌐⌐⌐⌐⌐⌐⌐⌐ *December 23, 2003*

A Wish
One More Magic Christmas

few days ago as I hung holiday decorations, my daughter asked, "Daddy,
Santa really real?"

Her two older brothers had been filling her head with doubts again.
Do you believe he's real?" I asked, stalling. She nodded vigorously, blonde
ngs bouncing up and down.

"Then he must be real," I said. And that reassurance, lame as it was,
emed to suffice. She informed me she would be putting out four cook-
s this year instead of the customary three because Santa had emptied the
ate last Christmas. Then she skipped happily off to write him a letter.

Colleen is 6, in first grade, our youngest child—and somehow no

longer a baby. If I had any say in the matter, I'd still be feeding her war
bottles and counting my success by the velocity of her burps.

But in this I have no say.

She is moving from the nest like an ocean liner moves from the doc
slowly but with unstoppable momentum. Tug on the mooring lines
you want; it will do no good. On the horizon, adulthood beckons.

Her older brothers, 11 and 10, have moved through the same stages b
fore her. But because she is our last, the passage is all the more bittersw
All I can say is thank god for video cameras.

With each hurdle she leaps, another chapter in that book called chi
hood closes forever. Like any good book, I don't want it to end.

Last Stop: Goodwill

As she reaches each benchmark—first step, first word, first school day
my wife and I at once cheer and sigh. We capture the moment on ta
and try to ignore those little stabbing pangs of loss.

Last spring, Colleen decided she was done with training wheels. I
moved them from her bike and spent the weekend running up and dov
our street beside her, holding her by the seat as she fought for balan
Out of sheer exhaustion, I finally let go—and was amazed, and just a lit
sad, to see her ride down the block without me, not once looking back

When her big brothers mastered bicycles, the training wheels went
the next in line. But this time they went to Goodwill. That era of our liv
is over.

It was the same for the stroller and the crib and the booster seat,
rendered obsolete seemingly overnight, reminders of how quickly bab
grow to children and children grow to teenagers and teenagers lea
home.

The day she learned to say "John" instead of "Wahn" nearly broke r
heart.

I try not to be too sentimental about these things. Spring turns to sur
mer, kids grow up. Believe me, the day I changed my final diaper will

wn as one of the unequivocally happiest of my life. What can I say?
me stages are easier to let go of than others. You can imagine how bro-
1 up I am that no one screams to watch Barney anymore.

I'm counting the years until I can get one of those "I'm spending my
ls' inheritance" bumper stickers.

The Art of Letting Go

id yet.

Parents are meant to prepare their children for the outside world, to
ke them strong and independent. So why am I feeling left out because
one needs me to tie shoes anymore?

I mentioned this to a woman friend of mine, and she asked, "So men
ve those feelings, too?" Yeah, I guess sometimes we do, at least when
re's nothing good on ESPN.

My friend Joe Schwerdt, a father of three boys, confessed to feeling the
ne tug. His youngest, Andrew, is the family's last to play Little League,
d father and son have been practicing. But each toss of the ball carries a
minder of what soon will pass. "He's my last boy and I'm hanging onto
childhood as long as I can," my friend wrote me. "I fear on the day he
ns 13 he'll suddenly discover the generation gap, put his baseball glove
ay, and put on a pair of headphones."

This holiday I want just one gift. And that is for my youngest to
1eeze a final magic Christmas out of her childhood—to have one more
ar of wonderment, of believing in jolly elves and prancing reindeer
th no other purpose in life but to spread generosity and joy.

Come Christmas morning, I will be up before dawn, video camera in
nd, to capture my daughter's face as she races to check the plate of
okies. I'm betting Santa will have eaten every last one.

For Teen Mother, the Son Is Rising

In her low-slung jeans and powder-blue sneakers, Kate Gowen could
any high school senior—except for one small detail. On her lap sits a
month-old baby boy.

His name is Donovan, named after the quarterback. The one-tir
North Penn High School student became pregnant with him shortly aft
she turned 16. And now, not quite a year and a half later, she realizes h
carefree—and, she admits, wild—childhood is officially behind her.

Yet she tells you this baby in all likelihood saved her life, literally—fro
jail, a drug overdose, or worse. And given her self-destructive path befo
his birth, you can believe it.

Sitting with Donovan in the small apartment in Hatfield that she shar
with her mother, Kate admits she was about as difficult as teenagers con
Starting at age 14, she tried just about everything.

She disappeared overnight, stole her mother's car, ran away from hon
skipped school for weeks at a time, experimented with alcohol and dru₃
and became sexually active.

"I was a total pothead," she says. "I fell in with a group of kids. We h
this 'the world is against us' mentality."

She threatened suicide several times and ended up in the mental-hea₁
system. "I never wanted to die," she now says, "but it was a real attenti∢
grabber."

Her mother, a single parent working as a waitress and dealing wi
her own personal problems, was unable to control the girl. "She w
very angry," Laura Gowen said.

By age 15, Kate found herself in an alternative school for troubl
teens. She lasted two months before pulling a knife on a student, getti
expelled and hauled into Montgomery County juvenile court. A jud

ed her on home probation. Within hours she had run away again, and
time the judge locked her up for 22 days.

Kate, a thin girl with long dark hair and pretty eyes, is not sure why she
so angry. She had never known her father, but her childhood in the
urbs was otherwise fully ordinary.

"I just had this image of myself as this hardened, tough girl," she says.

On Halloween 2002, a month after her 16th birthday, she learned she
pregnant. After three anguished weeks, with nearly everyone she
w urging her to have an abortion, Kate made her decision.

"I just couldn't live with terminating this pregnancy," she said. "And I
ldn't see myself carrying him for nine months and then just giving
up. So I decided to keep him."

The pregnancy landed her at a place that she says profoundly changed
life for the better—the Lakeside Pregnancy and Parenting Center, a
profit, private school for teenage mothers in Fort Washington.

t was small, just 30 students, and the counselors and teachers worked
nsely with her. They showered her with attention, teaching life skills,
ing her to doctor's appointments, and pushing her academically.
Mostly, they just believed in her.

"Kate is very bright," Nancy Kane, the school's director, told me. "As
as IQ, she is a gifted kid."

ince Donovan's birth in July, Kate has made a "huge turnaround,"
e said, and thrown herself into parenting and schoolwork. Once con-
red at high risk for dropping out, she is back on track to graduate
h her North Penn classmates in June.

Kate says she has been sober since the day she learned she was preg-
t, and she is proud that she delivered a healthy, 9-pound baby.

She says she avoids her old crowd and finds friendship now in the
er young moms she has met. After graduation, she plans to pursue
sing.

Life won't be easy, but it has a new purpose. And a joy, as well.

"My son is the driving force in my life," she says. "He's everything. He's helped me turn from a melodramatic teenager headed to a grave or a cell into someone worth respecting."

She lifts him over her head and adds: "I owe everything to him, I'm working my hardest to give him the wonderful life he deserves."

April 12, 20

Mother Keeps the Passion Alive

Christine Detwiler, teacher and mother, stands before a group of stud at North Penn High School near Lansdale and tries to explain why sh putting up $100 of her own money as a prize for an essay contest.

You see, she tells them, "My son, Ben, was once a student here, to And then she adds in a calm, even voice she has had 13 years to pract "He died when he was a junior."

It was the night of October 26, 1991, and Ben, 16, and a friend w walking home along Route 309 from the Montgomery Mall in No Wales, where Ben worked baking cinnamon rolls.

The distance was less than a mile, and the boys were walking in grass, neither of which made any difference in the end. A drunken dri veered off the road, killing Ben instantly. She was convicted and senten to three years in prison.

Life is filled with little ironies. And one that will always haunt B mother is the fact that she would not permit Ben to drive until he 18, figuring she could keep him safe that way.

Detwiler, an elementary school teacher in the North Penn distr mentions none of this to the students before her. Rather, she tells th what kind of a boy her son was—an idealist, an activist, a thinker, an talker who loved to debate issues.

"He was also a pretty good writer," she tells the students.

A Better World

ıd that is why, shortly after his death, seeking some positive outlet in
hich to pour her bottomless grief, she established the Ben Detwiler
riting Contest for juniors at the school. Ben once wrote that his goal
ıs to make the world a better place, and that is the theme for the con-
t, now in its 13th year.

She continues to sponsor the event, Detwiler later told me, as a way of
eping her son's memory alive—a way of holding on to him for just a
tle longer. "I want young people to do the active thinking about their
orld that Ben can no longer do," she said.

Ben, she tells you, was the kind of kid who navigated adolescence out-
le the mainstream. He was small for his age and not athletic, and by the
ne he reached high school he was cultivating a punk-rock appearance,
eing his hair black and wearing it in a spiked Mohawk cut. He pierced
nose, wore black leather, and played guitar in a rock band.

Because of his look, many students and parents assumed he was trouble
st avoided. Being ostracized by some taught him early lessons about
ejudice and stereotypes. It also led him into an unexpected friendship
th an unlikely ally, the school's principal, Juan Baughn, an African
nerican who himself knew the sting of being outside the majority. The
o spent many hours after school talking and debating—and, Baughn
ints out, coming to respect each other.

A Shared Pain

t hurt him, the disapproval," said Baughn, who is now an assistant
ıools superintendent in Washington, DC. "It just blew him away that
ople were not more receptive to who he was inside instead of just what
looked like. At one point, Ben said to me, 'Dr. Baughn, you know what
like?' And I did, and I do."

The former principal was happy to hear Ben's mother has kept the es-
contest going. "He was a little guy with a great big heart," Baughn

said. "He wanted to save the world. I kept talking to him about saving piece of it."

And so again this year, a group of North Penn juniors who we just toddlers when Ben died will try their hand at capturing that sa passion.

They will write about war and poverty and, perhaps, about accepti those who don't look like they do.

The winner will take home a plaque and a check. And the mother she is lucky, might catch a glimpse of her son in their words.

His classmates are adults now, with careers and marriages and kids their own. They have moved on, and so has Ben's mother, as best she c

But a part of her remains frozen in the fall of her son's junior ye That's how she sees him still, a vulnerable teen with a great big hea searching for his place in this world.

"Right now he would be 29," she says in that voice of hers, the callu of time cushioning a mother's grief. "I have a son who will always be 1

July 13, 20

Getaway Becomes Dad-Son Mind Trip

A 12-year-old mind is a strange and beautiful thing to behold.

And when I drove into the dawn with my son recently for a four-c backpacking trip in the Allegheny National Forest, I got to behold mc than I would wish on any parent. There was no mom, no little brother sister. Only the two of us.

The kid just would not shut up.

To help pass the six-hour drive, I had brought along a large supply favorite tunes—my music, not his, of course. But he kept turning do the volume so he could chat my ear off.

"You just turned down Jimi Hendrix," I admonished. "Don't y know it's a sin to turn down Jimi Hendrix?"

Dad, you always play it too loud."

That's not possible," I retorted.

He eased the volume down. There were questions galore that needed
vering.

Hey, Dad, if Mars veered off course and crashed into Earth, what do
think would happen?"

That's impossible," I said.

But what if it wasn't? Then what?"

I have no idea," I said, "but I'm pretty sure you'd use it as an excuse to
out of doing homework."

Next question: "If you had to eat poison, what kind would you pick?"

I would never eat poison—and neither should you."

But let's just say you had to."

refused to answer on the grounds that no father should be endorsing
c substances. But he wouldn't relent. "I don't know," I finally said.
mlock?" I figured if it worked for Socrates, it worked for me.

Weird and Evil

hat's the weirdest thing ever?"

You?"

That's not funny." Two-second pause, and then: "Who's the most evil
on in all of history?"

Easy," I said.

And it can't be Hitler."

I was going to say Hitler."

Everyone says Hitler. That's too easy. Someone other than Hitler."

nd so went the long drive. I was tempted to duct-tape the boy's
ith shut—a disciplinary measure for which there is ample precedent
in our region. And I just might have tried it, except for this one
g: He's 12 and still thinks his father holds the answers to all mysteries.
t year he will be 13, officially a teenager, and things no doubt will be
rent.

By 13, he'll consider me somewhere between mold spores and p
scum on the spectrum of valued information sources. I thought I'd be
enjoy the babble while I could. He's talking now, I told myself, let I
Soon enough he just might go silent, and then I'd be kicking myself.

So I rolled down the windows to breathe in the country smell
mowed hay and cow manure and let the inquisition continue.

His mind was a preadolescent cauldron of popping, snapping, crack
synapses, and it jumped all over as he chased his curiosity.

What was the worst disaster? The biggest crime? Coolest invention

Politics and Presidents

"Who's your favorite Republican?"

"Ever?"

"Ever."

"Abraham Lincoln."

"Favorite Democrat?" he asked.

"Harry Truman."

"Who's the most famous person you've ever met?"

"Frank Zappa."

"Who's he?"

"Oy. Kids nowadays."

"Who else who's famous?"

"I interviewed the first George Bush once," I said.

"Really? Was he nice?"

"Very nice."

"Were you nervous?" he asked.

"Just a little."

"Too cool," he said.

The questions and answers continued through our hike deep into
woods, through dinner on a ledge overlooking a fast-moving brook,
through the fire's dying embers.

I was beat, but I dared not stop him, knowing in a year, or perhaps

nonth, he would be cringing at his father's glory-days' tales of close en-
.inters with dead rock stars and past presidents. For now he was all ears,
1 I was too cool. I'd take it.

As the moon rose over the trees, I finally managed to get in a question
my own. "So, kiddo," I asked. "What do you say we go to sleep now?"

⟶ *March 7, 2005*

Brain-Damaged but Still a "Gift"

r name is Millie.

She came into this world 55 years ago, a healthy, chubby baby with a
•ck of dark hair. Her family loved her then, and despite everything—or
'haps because of it—loves her now even more.

Millie Reynolds has never spoken a word or returned a smile. Her first
tative baby steps would be her last. Just before her first birthday in
50, she contracted viral meningitis, with sustained fevers that left her
foundly brain-damaged.

The doctors said an institution would be best, but Millie's parents
uld not listen. They brought their damaged baby home to the Olney
tion of Philadelphia and lovingly cared for her as she grew, unaware,
n a child to an adolescent to an adult.

Today her world is a small bedroom on the second floor of the Chel-
ham home of her older brother, Charles Reynolds, and his wife, Susan,
o took over Millie's 24/7 care after the parents' deaths. For the last 17
rs, the couple have dedicated their lives to her without regret.

'She is our forever baby," Susan Reynolds says, gazing upon Millie lying
le-eyed but unseeing beneath a picture of Jesus. And Millie is.

She requires diapers and total care. Until four years ago, when a feeding
e was surgically inserted as her swallowing reflex weakened, she sucked
k from a bottle and was spoon-fed pureed fruits and vegetables.

A Child's Face

She is blind, and paralyzed from the neck down. Her hands curl
against her wrists, and her spine over the years has taken the shape o
curving mountain road. She weighs just 80 pounds, and with her soft sk
and black hair not showing a strand of gray, she looks almost like
teenager, even a child.

Ask her family whether Millie's life has value or meaning, if the kind
course might not be to simply remove the feeding tube so she can esca
the prison of her broken body, and they just smile.

"Millie is a gift," Susan Reynolds, a third-grade teacher, says. "Her l
has brought many blessings to our family."

Adds her husband, a furniture salesman: "She has taught us the imp
tance of life."

The couple are devout Catholics, and caring for Millie has cemen
their conviction that all life, even one as compromised as this, is precio

They say Millie has taught them charity, patience, and unqualified lo
She has shown them what really matters in life. Most important, they
her continual presence has given their three now-grown children
greatest gift of all—compassion.

Not bad for a human life many would dismiss as better off dead.

In exchange, they give her loving, dignified care. They point
proudly that Millie's doctors are in awe that she has never suffered a sin
bedsore in 54 years.

Who Decides?

The Reynoldses have followed with interest—and dismay—the natio
uproar over Terri Schiavo, the brain-damaged former Huntingdon Va
woman whose feeding tube, a judge ruled last week, could be remove
early as March 18.

What is missing from the debate, they believe, is a simple but fun
mental question: Whose right is it, anyway, to decide what constitute

worth living? Can any human really make that decision about an-
er?

The Reynoldses believe not.

Despite what some medical ethicists say, they do not see Millie's feed-
 tube as an artificial means to prolong life but simply as a medical tool
allow her to more comfortably and safely get the sustenance all humans
d. Before the tube, she had aspirated food into her lungs, leading to
tical bouts of pneumonia.

When Millie's time comes—and she grows weaker each year—they
l not order any extraordinary measures to prolong life. But neither will
y ever consider steps to shorten it. That decision, they believe, is be-
en Millie and a higher authority.

"Our faith and our love, that's what has guided us," Susan Reynolds says.
As she talks, her forever baby rocks her head from side to side, her
gue out slightly, her sightless gaze far away in that netherworld the rest
us will never comprehend, somewhere between here and forever gone.

April 15, 2005

Speeder Dad Learns an Important Lesson

vas one of those amazing spring days that demand a drive in the coun-
 The sun was brilliant, the sky a cloudless blue, the earth's awakening
ll sweet on the air.

"Hop in," I told the kids. "We're taking a ride." A ride to nowhere and
 no purpose other than to feel the wind in our faces and to take in the
-popping beauty of budding maples and blossoming cherry trees.

We found our way to one of those bucolic Bucks County country
ds that artists draw. We whizzed past cows and barns and pastures, the
roof open, the windows down, and Stevie Wonder on the stereo. Bliss.
Then I glanced in my rearview mirror. Bliss be gone.

A police car was tight on my tail, lights flashing, siren wailing. A cho[...] swear word nearly escaped my lips before I remembered the kids and [...] tered, "Shoot. Golldarnitall!"

With sinking heart, I pulled over, knowing I had been having way t[...] much fun not to have been speeding. But the cop whizzed by me, inst[...] pulling over the pickup truck I had been following. Whew, better h[...] than me, I thought.

My good fortune was short lived. The state trooper, it turned out, [...] going for a double play. He waved me over behind the pickup. I hand[...] him my driver's license.

"Mr. Grogan, are you in a hurry today?" he asked.

"Actually, no," I said.

No Good Excuses

I wanted to tell him about the joyous riot of spring, the blue sky, the bu[...] ding trees, the awakening earth, and all that. I wanted to extol the wind[...] my face and the unadulterated pleasure of Stevie Wonder and an op[...] sunroof on a day so perfect—neither too hot nor too cold—it could h[...] been delivered by angels. But I was pretty sure the *joie de vivre* defe[...] was not going to cut it.

"You were driving 62 in a 40-mph zone," he told me. And then he [...] livered the most withering blow of all: "And with children in the car!"

His tone was a cross of contempt and concern, and the wo[...] stung. What kind of a father would go speeding around curves w[...] his own flesh-and-blood beside him? The only good news was t[...] the guy in the pickup had been going even faster—and he had [...] kid along, too.

The punishment for my lead-footed indiscretion: a $160 fine and th[...] points on my driving record. But that was nothing compared to w[...] awaited me when I glanced at the face of my 8-year-old daughter in [...] backseat. My son, 12, was more amused than anything by my predi[...] ment. But Colleen looked stricken.

was her dad. And to a second grader, that meant I was her
_, her compass, her rock of stability and righteousness. I was the
 who kept her safe, who always told her the police were there
·rotect her from bad people. I was the guy who regularly admon-
·d her to obey the rules and do the right thing, even when no one
 watching.

·nd here I was, caught red-handed on the wrong side of the law.

Off the Pedestal

·it was only a speeding ticket, but I could see it on her face, the dawn-
· awareness that her father was less than perfect, was in fact something
·oaching criminal.

·he trooper seemed to see it, too, and in a softer tone said, "We're just
·1g to keep everyone safe."

·nd then to Colleen: "I'm glad to see you all wearing your seatbelts."

·ler face brightened. See, her dad wasn't a total bum!

· thanked the officer—why, I'm not quite sure—and drove off with all
·zip of a church lady on her way to Sunday services.

· have preached ad nauseam to my kids that actions have consequences,
· now I was Exhibit A.

·I learned an important lesson today," I told them. "The rules are there
·a reason, and I broke them, and now I have to pay."

·'s odd, this family affair. We spend the first half of our lives hiding our
·erfections from our parents so as not to disappoint them, and we
·d the second half hiding them from our children for the same reason.
·)n this achingly lovely day, I had no place to hide. My little game
·up.

·peeder Dad was guilty as charged.

⁓ *April 25, 2*

Introducing a Gift Named Danny

Friday was the day Susan Haggerty had apprehensively awaited for we Her coming-out day.

Nerves on edge, she walked into her son Jack's fourth-grade class a Alphonsus in Maple Glen, Montgomery County. Jack greeted his mo at the door and then returned to his seat, surrounded by his classmate

He, too, was ready for this moment. Some teasing had begun. S< things had been said. It was time.

His mother paused in front of the class, took a breath and then "Jack has a brother. Jack's brother has autism."

There. It was said.

Not that Haggerty had hidden the fact, but some things are harde talk about than others. This was her first time standing before a grou this size to disclose her son's autism.

She asked the children whether they knew what that word meant, one bespectacled girl shot up her hand and said, "It's like you're kin out of control sometimes."

"They have a problem with their brains," said another.

"You've been reading up!" the mother praised her.

In simple sentences, she told Danny's story. He was a beautiful n born, perfect in every way. But his parents began to notice he was not the other babies. He did not cry like they did, did not chatter, did achieve the same milestones.

Different Drummers

In 1998, when Danny was 2, the parents received the formal diagnosi

What she wanted the students to know is that children such as Da while different, are not to be feared. Sometimes they grunt; someti

y flap their arms or get right in your face. They have a hard time look-
 in your eyes. But they mean no harm.

'If you're not afraid of them, you might find out they're nice guys," she
s the children, "They want to have friends, too."

This coming out as an autism parent is not meant just for the children,
 for their parents, too. She gives each child a two-page letter to take
ne. In it, Haggerty bares her soul.

'We had the usual expectations and dreams that parents have for
ir children," she wrote. "On this particular day [when Danny was
gnosed], everything in the world changed for my husband and me."

And she told them something else—that Danny is not the only one in
ir home with autism. His younger brother, Will, 7, has been diagnosed
h a milder form of the condition.

She apologized if her children disturb anyone at Sunday Mass. "We
it you to know how much we appreciate your patience and kindness,"
 concluded.

Separate and Apart

er Haggerty finished her talk, as the children streamed out of class,
 confessed that life as the parent of autistic children can be lonely
l isolated. The invitations to socialize are painfully few, she said,
ling, "I've learned to grow a tougher skin."

But she and her husband now know what really matters, and most of it
sts within the four walls of a family's home.

She has discovered that sometimes amazing gifts come in surprising
kages. Sometimes they are wrapped in heartbreak.

Before Friday's presentation at St. Alphonsus, Haggerty took me to
•ther school a few blocks away, Maple Glen Elementary, where I met
 gift that is Danny.

He charged into the room, arms aflutter, eyes darting, and smashed his
 against his mother's.

He is a beautiful, freckle-faced boy with watery blue eyes who spe
in two- and three-word sentences, which makes his mother beam w
pride. Just months ago, he was limited to one-word responses.

Thinking he is going home, he says, "I get backpack. My tumi
rumbles."

He cannot tell me his age—nine, but he knows what he will do wh
he gets home. It's the same thing he does every day

"Rewind!" he squeals.

And that is what he literally will do, over and over again: rewi
videotapes, their soothing whir comforting him. His mother laug
hugs him. He prances off like a stallion.

Jack's brothers have autism. This family is through apologizing.

May 6, 20

When a Child Goes Missing

It had the makings of every parent's worst nightmare—a missing child.

My best friend from college was visiting with his wife and two daug
ters. I loaded them and my three children into the minivan for a tour
historic Bethlehem. One second we were nosing our way through co
nial-era ruins along a fast-moving river; the next I was yelling, "Whe
Conor?"

My middle child, who was 7 at the time, had simply disappeared. "
was just here a second ago," my friend Pete Kelly said.

His wife, Maureen, gathered up the other children, and Pete an
searched the area. As the minutes ticked by, I focused ever more frantic
on two scenarios. One involved the icy river with its rapids and jag
boulders; the other involved a man who had been playing with a pur
nearby and now was gone, too.

Pete, a police officer in Michigan, seemed to be having the sa

ughts. I trotted along the riverbank, peering with dread into the water;
dodged in and out of old foundations and buildings, anywhere some-
e could pull a child.

After 20 minutes, we met up again. "Nothing," he said.

I looked at him, not wanting to say what I was thinking. He was the
p; I trusted his judgment.

"I think it's time to call 911," he said.

He ran to a store to find a phone; I returned to the stream. Two
nutes later, I heard his shouts from a block away, and when I
ned, he held my son above his head.

Relief and Gratitude

lief, so intense I felt my legs wobble, washed over me.

Conor had wandered out of sight, and when he couldn't find us he did
actly what I had taught him to do: He returned to the car to wait for
There he was when Pete reached the street, sitting on the curb, bravely
hting back tears.

If only the family of Jamil Guy could have had such a happy ending.

The 13-year-old drowned in Chester Creek on Monday after he and
two cousins tried to turn a small, plastic wading pool into a boat.

They were supposed to be at their grandmother's house, but they
d sneaked down to the creek across from Chester High School.
ey were boys being boys. Boys doing what boys have always done
d always will.

Jamil Guy's death stopped me short and made me appreciate my lucky
w. It reminded me how differently my own son's disappearance could
e turned out—at the bottom of a river or, lured by a cute puppy, in
trunk of a predator's car.

Jamil's death pointed out what every parent knows but tries not to
ate on—that no matter how vigilant you try to be, you cannot watch
m every second of every day, especially as they grow into teens. As

much as you try to teach them to act responsibly, you cannot cont
their actions.

Ascribing Blame

And yet something the boy's family said after his death bothered n
Family members were upset that the boys were able to make their w
down the steep embankment to the water.

"If there had been a fence up there, they wouldn't have gone t
route," Jamil's aunt, Janet Guy, told reporters.

A grieving aunt can be forgiven for seeking a scapegoat on whom
blame this tragedy.

For dreaming there is someone out there—government, society, son
body—capable of wailing our children away from danger.

But it would have to be a mighty wall and an endless one, too, lc
enough and high enough and impenetrable enough to protect every ch
from every conceivable hazard.

From every creek and pond and railroad track and cliff and lurki
stranger.

If only there had been a fence . . .

If only it were that simple.

It is easy for parents whose children are safe today to pass judgment.
say Jamil and his cousins should have been more closely supervis
should have been better trained to avoid danger. I won't be among the

I've had my brush with the fenceless world and know this: Jamil co
have been Conor and Conor Jamil. One boy's tragedy, another's close c

In life, there are no foolproof fences, no impervious cocoons. Only l
tle children and the adults who do their best to keep them safe.

"It's Never the Same"
Too True

as running late.

At the end of the long hallway, the last room on the right sat empty.

The bed was made, a walker in the corner. My mother and her
eelchair were missing.

I found a nurse. "I'm Ruth Grogan's son. Is my mother around?"

It was a dumb question. This was a nursing home. Of course she was
und. Everyone was always around.

"I'd try the chapel," the nurse offered. "Mass started at 11."

Life has its chapters, distinct divisions marked by watershed events, and
s summer marked a new one in mine. A year earlier, when I had visited
aging parents at their home outside Detroit, ripe tomatoes lined the
ndowsill, a pot of soup simmered on the stove, and my folks greeted me
pily at the door.

This summer's visit marked a new beginning. As my children swam in
lake I had swum in as a boy, I sifted through my father's papers, visited
grave, and spent time with my mother in the place she now calls
me.

As far as nursing homes go, it's a lovely one, perched on a shaded hill
rlooking a lake and run by kind nuns committed to compassionate
e. But it is still a nursing home with all the smells and sounds and sad-
s nursing homes hold.

I made my way down corridors lined with frail women passing the
rs. "Take me with you," one of them pleaded as I passed.

Bowed White Heads

the chapel, an ancient priest celebrated Mass before a small clutch of

nuns and about three dozen patients, their wheelchairs arranged in an
around the altar. From behind, the bowed white heads all looked alike.
I scanned the congregates, I realized nearly all of them were asleep. M
mother was no exception.

I touched her shoulder and whispered, "Hi, Ruthie." Her eyes oper
and widened with surprise. She had forgotten I was coming.

My 89-year-old mother's memory has been fleeing her for some ye
now. When my father died in December, she lost not only her husband
58 years but a devoted and exceptionally attentive 24/7 caregiver.

Mom's eyes shut again, and I stood with my hands on her shoulder
the priest soldiered on. At Communion, he walked down the rows
wheelchairs, placing wheat hosts onto tongues. My mother woke to
cept hers and, as she always has, pressed a fist to her heart and beg
working her lips in silent prayer.

Some things are not easily lost.

After Mass, I wheeled her into the courtyard, where she tilted her h
toward the sun and smiled. Deep lines crossed her face, and her hair wa
snowy as a blizzard. But a child's face looked up at me, a little girl lost
her innocence.

A Song from Long Ago

She began to hum and then sing. It was a song I had never heard befc
a ditty about a brash child swallowed by an alligator she thought
could tame. Mom had no idea what she had eaten for breakfast t
morning, but she reeled effortlessly through the stanzas, not missin
beat.

"Where did you learn that?" I asked.

"Girl Scouts," she said.

I had to laugh. "That was 80 years ago! It's about time you sang it
me." Then she sang it all over again.

We sat quietly for a moment. She broke the silence with an
servation.

"Once they leave home, that's it," she volunteered as if she were telling someone other than one of those who had left. "They come back to , but it is never the same."

wanted to insist otherwise, but she was right. It never is. It never was. wheeled her back to her room and kissed her goodbye.

I'll be back this evening with Jenny and the kids," I told her. What d not say is that the next morning we would be returning to nsylvania.

Outside in the parking lot, I looked back through her room window re I had left her. She was peering out at something far, far away. When ught her attention, a startled look of pleasant surprise came across her , the same look she had given me at chapel. It was as if she were see-me for the first time.

Aw, Mom," I whispered.

he blew me a kiss. I blew one back, then drove away.

⌐⌐⌐ *October 17, 2005*

Who's a Father? A Guy Who's There

ticed them immediately.

tanding in front of me in line at a fast-food restaurant near Souderton rain-streaked Tuesday, the father and his daughter were hard to miss. o a stranger's eye at first glance, they did not appear as if they be-ed together.

he was 6 or 7, a pretty, delicate girl with sand-colored hair that fell to shoulders. She was dressed sharply in a blue-and-green plaid jumper, te shirt, white anklets, and black dress shoes.

Ie was about 35, dressed in old jeans, a sleeveless T-shirt, and a ball cap n backward over a bandana tied around his head. Both forearms ted large tattoos, and his face, dominated by a long mustache and ggly goatee, spoke of a hard life. He used bad grammar.

He looked as if he belonged on a big Harley-Davidson, not here
line with a schoolgirl.

I don't even know for a fact that he was her father, but the longe
watched them, the more convinced of it I became. They had that cert
easy chemistry that can exist between dads and their little girls.

They stood quietly in line, not talking. He rested his muscled arms
the counter; she leaned into him. He ordered their food, adding, "and
of them frosty things" for the girl.

A Comfortable Silence

They sat a few tables from me and ate mostly in silence, but it was a co
fortable, easy silence. He reached over and unwrapped her cheesebur;
She swung her legs beneath her as she chewed.

I noted with approval that he held back her frozen dessert until she
finished her meal. Then he sprinkled the topping on it a little at a tim
she ate so each bite would be special.

It might say something about my own prejudices and stereotypes th
took notice of this rough-hewn, working-class guy simply meeting
minimum standards we'd expect of any parent. If he were dressed i
khaki suit and penny loafers, would I have looked twice?

I hope so. The special one-on-one bond between fathers and t
daughters is one of life's more underreported joys. And one worthy
notice.

When my daughter was a preschooler, I sometimes took her ou
breakfast before work, just the two of us. No Mom Rules. We
with our fingers, shared drinks from the same straw, and burped v
abandon. Moments worth remembering after others have faded i
dusk.

What struck me about this father and daughter was how effortle
they interacted. He was not one of those smothering "quality-time" ty
jabbering and treating his child like a miniature adult at a cocktail par

But he was there for her, and she for him. It was something to wat

Little Life Lessons

er the man and girl were done eating, he walked her to the bathroom
l stood outside the door until she came out. She held her hands up to
nose so he could smell the soap, proof she had washed them.

At the door to the parking lot, she pulled. "Push," he said.

She pushed, the door swung open, and she looked up at him as if he
re the smartest man alive.

As they stepped outside, it occurred to me that parenting is not
ket science. You don't need a doctoral degree in child development
be decent at it.

Sometimes it is as simple as saying push instead of pull.

Fathers, I was reminded, come in many shapes and sizes and fit no one
ld. The good ones have a few things in common, and at the top of the
is just being there. Present and accounted for. There for the big mo-
nts, but also there for burgers at Wendy's on a rainy afternoon.

They stood beneath the awning for a moment, surveying the puddle-
·d parking lot. The girl looked down at her new shoes, and then the
n did, too. Without a word, he leaned over and scooped her up in one
ng, tattooed arm. She tossed her arms around his neck, peachy cheek
ornery bristle, and together they headed off into the dampness.

She was with her dad, high and dry and safe in his arms. Did life for a
e girl in a plaid jumper get any better than this?

August 21, 2006

Learn the Rhythm of Solitude
A Backpack Hike Shows Grace that Comes in Solitude

he summer of 1977, I nearly sent my poor mother into cardiac arrest
en I announced my plans to hitchhike and backpack around New
land by myself.

"Alone?" Mom asked. "Oh no, you aren't."

"Mom," I shot back in my best this-time-you're-not-winning voi "I'm going."

She began to protest, but my father caught her eye. He didn't breath word, but his face said it all. I know he's your baby. I know you worry. I he's not a child anymore. You need to let go.

My father knew what dwells in a young man's heart. He knew t sometimes a guy has to find adventure to find himself.

I had just finished my sophomore year of college and had a few wee until my summer job started. I had hitchhiked and backpacked w friends before. Who knows what I was trying to prove, but this tim needed to do it alone.

When my father was 20, he was supporting a widowed mother a two younger siblings as he worked his way through college. Not lo after, he was on an aircraft carrier in the South Pacific. He did need a solo road trip to prove his chops. But he seemed to und stand that I did.

"Well, OK, then," my mother finally said. "But you better call."

We made a deal. I would phone every other day, and Mom would k her worrying to herself.

I set out with everything I needed on my back. My first night ou was ready to raise the white flag and go limping home.

I had gotten dropped off at a trailhead of the Appalachian Trail western Massachusetts. Evening was fast approaching, and I hiked only a couple of miles before setting up camp. Rather than put up tent, I decided to sleep under the stars. As blackness enveloped coyotes began yipping all around. I swore I could hear them mov through the brush.

Then the rain started. I pulled a tarp over me and figured that wo keep me dry enough. What seemed like hours later, I bolted awa rainwater rushing in from where it had pooled atop the tarp. I soaked.

reached for my watch and hoped daybreak was imminent. The illu-
ated hands read 11:20 p.m. It was going to be a very long night.

t the first gray of dawn, I rose, wrung as much water as I could from
sleeping bag, and began to walk. By lunch the sun was out, and I
ad my wet clothes and bedding over shrubs to dry. Yet my spirits re-
ned damp. The steep terrain left me winded and with aching muscles.
ters popped out on my feet. As much as I didn't want to admit it, I
miserable.

But I soldiered on, hiking through most of Massachusetts and into
mont. With each day, my strength and confidence grew. I fell into a
tine, rising with the sun, hiking until it began to slant low in the sky,
stopping to swim, cook over a small open fire, and fall asleep to the
turnal sounds of nature.

he rhythm of solitude, once so intimidating, began to feel comfort-
. Aloneness, I was learning, does not have to equal loneliness.

nd when I had walked as far as I cared to walk, I put out my thumb
began to hitch my way around New England, stopping in villages and
ege towns, eventually making it to Boston.

all the encounters with strangers, I came across just one creep. An
y silent man who picked me up and when we reached my turnoff
red to drive me 20 miles out of his way if I'd only pose for a few
tos. When I balked, he assured me they would just be snapshots of
standing beside the car. Why not, I figured. I was so clueless, it never
rred to me why he might be so motivated to collect photos of
ng strangers.

ut he was the exception.

here was the young hippie girl who picked me up in a Volk-
gen microbus (yes, stereotypes come from somewhere) and
ed a cooler of vegetable sandwiches and cold beer with me.
re were the graduate students in Amherst who fed me a big
hetti dinner and let me sleep on their living room floor. There
the cop who found me with my thumb out on a desolate

stretch of road and pulled a U-turn to give me a lift to a m
traveled intersection. And the small-town folks everywhere who
fered me cold drinks as I passed by.

For all the bad things in this world, I was learning a fundamental tr
that people are basically good and kind and generous. You couldn'
dumb about it, but if you took a chance on them, the vast majority wc
not betray your trust.

That summer I came to appreciate the beauty of solitude and the
of companionship. I learned to revel in nature and trust my instincts. M
important, I came to believe in the overarching decency of the hur
race.

Not a bad haul for one young man's summer sojourn.

Animals

What's Good for the Goose? Us

been talking to the geese lately.

"You guys," I say. "What's your problem? Can't you do any better than
? Shouldn't you be basking on a nice golf course in Florida?"

They look up at me like I'm some kind of quack and say what they al-
s say. Honk!

Canada geese. The big, fat, beautiful birds are everywhere, ubiquitous
aments on the suburban landscape. I pass them as I walk into the mall,
e by the cemetery, take my kids to the playground, visit college cam-
es and corporate parks, and turn into my neighborhood.

A whole big flock of them has taken over the lawn outside the door of
office, where they chew the frozen grass, ignoring the stream of hu-
s trudging by just feet away.

What I don't get is why here? Greater Philadelphia has its virtues, but
wild and scenic refuge for water fowl, it's got to be near the bottom
he list. Especially in March with the snow, the ice, the salt, and that
npy bulky-sweater look.

've been trying to talk some sense into them. But do they listen? You
ıld think they were teenagers.

"Excuse me," I tell them. "If I could fly to New Orleans for free, do
think I'd be standing here in a slush pile eating frozen grass? Hello?
've got wings. Use them."

Honk!

Flap Southward, Dummies

"Look, I'll make it easy for you. I'll point, and you fly. It's not that co plicated. South is that way. Just keep going until you hit Disney World. on. Shoo!"

Honk!

"All right. If you're not going to fly south for winter like any self-specting goose would do, at least hang out at Valley Forge or some ot open space. I mean, is a grimy industrial zone along the Schuylkill re your idea of a good time?"

It's no use. They just keep chewing and pooping, chewing and poopi

I turn for help to a water-fowl professional, none other than the app priately named Donald Drake, a wildlife specialist and assistant profes of wildlife management at Rutgers University.

Professor Drake, first things first. Is that really your name?

Absolutely, he assures me.

So how come these dumb geese insist on hanging out in the Ph deep freeze when they can be catching rays on Hilton Head Island?

Drake does not duck the question.

What we see around the 'burbs are not migratory geese, he expla We see their plumper couch-potato cousins, which are so happy h they've made this their year-round home.

"They most likely never migrated a day in their life," Drake says.

And if they appear fearless, it's because they are, he says. The suburbs essentially a predator- and hunting-free zone for geese, and they've ured out that we suburbanites are harmless weenies. (Oh yeah? Let th try stepping in front of our SUVs as we head home from work!)

Creating an Ideal Habitat

We spend tens of thousands of dollars on everything from border co to firecrackers to shoo away the winged eating machines. But basic they don't give a flying quack.

Drake points out that we've given them everything a goose could pos-
ly ask for. "As Americans, we have a fascination with well-manicured
s," Drake says. And *Branta canadensis* thanks us for it.

Not only are our suburban lawns and soccer fields tasty, but we keep
m nice and short, just how geese like them so no enemies can sneak
on them. And then we dig backyard ponds and subdivision drainage
s, which they like, too. And we chase off most of the bird's natural
dators. Some of us even feed them bread.

We've pretty much given geese everything they could ask for ex-
t their own cable channel. And, remind me again, which species is
posed to have the superior intellect?

"Most of their life they spend grazing and just loafing around," Drake
. "People ask, 'Wouldn't it be great to have a dog's life?' But to have a
nada goose's life, I think, would be even better."

Right. And now if you'll excuse me, I need to get back out there and
their drink orders.

April 4, 2003

A Feline Air Traveler Lost in Philadelphia

x is MIA.

Missing in action, not on a battlefield in the Iraqi desert, but some-
ere in the cavernous bowels in Philadelphia International Airport.
Felix is a cat.

The black feline with the white patch on his chest disappeared March
uring a plane change in Philadelphia while en route from Baltimore to
ndon to join his owners. No one has seen a trace of him since.

U.S. Airways, which was transporting the cat, has put out food and
er, conducted several sweeps, posted Felix's photograph, even hired a
ker with a beagle to try to sniff the cat out of hiding. All to no avail.

His owners, while acknowledging that a lost feline is not exa
headline news, want him back desperately. So desperately that they h
traveled the Atlantic Ocean and back again in search of him.

The story begins in Baltimore with Rebecca Smith, a British nar
and her American husband, Darrell, an events planner. Earlier this year,
couple decided to return to England to be near Rebecca's parents.

Rebecca and the couple's 3-year-old daughter flew to London in J
uary. Darrell and Felix the cat were to follow later. Darrell made it; Fe
locked in a pet carrier bearing a large "Live Animal" sticker, did not.

U.S. Airways admits a mistake was made. Said spokeswoman A
Kudwa: "We continue our very diligent efforts to find the animal, [whi
at this time has not been found."

The Wrong Conveyor Belt

A baggage handler was supposed to take Felix to a cargo area to rec
food and water and await transfer. Instead, a cargo manager told
Smiths, the employee accidentally put Felix's carrier on a conveyor l
that took him on a journey into the airline's cavernous luggage area.

When workers finally located the carrier, the door was ajar, a
Felix was gone. "I just find it absolutely amazing that in a space
about 20 minutes they lost an 18-pound cat," Rebecca Smith, 34, t
me by telephone from England.

Three days after the disappearance, U.S. Airways flew the couple b
to Philadelphia and put them up in a hotel overnight so they could co
the baggage area to lure their shy cat out of hiding. Felix, if he was sti
the building, wasn't taking the bait.

"It was very much a wasted trip," Darrell Smith said. "We want our
back; that's the main thing. But I don't think that's going to happen.
been a month now."

While the airline insists the search continues, the Smiths se
otherwise.

I don't think they're really worried about it anymore," Darrell Smith

he Smiths said the airline has agreed to refund Felix's $257 ticket and told them to submit a bill for the price of the cat.

aid Rebecca Smith: "We got him from a shelter when he was two iths old. Monetarily, the cat has no value."

A Loyal Friend

to the family, Felix is a priceless family member. The big lazy cat ed Rebecca through many homesick nights in America and became a stant companion to the couple's daughter, Dominique. "It was like he guarding her," the wife said.

If it were lost clothing, we wouldn't care. You can replace clothing," said. Then, perhaps realizing how her concern for a cat might sound d the mounting human casualties of war, she added: "You can't really erstand unless you are a cat person."

Or at least a pet person. We know better, but still we treat them like dren, spoiling them, worrying over them, grieving when they die.

ellingly, the couple have begun to speak of their pet in the past tense, 1 as the relationship between the couple and U.S. Airways grows in-singly tense. The Smiths say airline officials are impatient with the ily's continued insistence on finding Felix. As for her part, Kudwa, the ne's spokeswoman, won't discuss details of the case, citing fear of a uit—a possibility the Smiths deny.

As hope for locating their pet of seven years fades, the couple has a re-st of the people of Philadelphia. If anyone spots a big black cat with a te tuft on his chest, please give a call.

here's a family across the ocean who very much wants him home n.

Saying Farewell to a Faithful Pal

In the gray of dawn, I found the shovel in the garage and walked dc
the hill to where the lawn meets the woods. There, beneath a wild che
tree, I began to dig.

The earth was loose and blessedly unfrozen, and the work went fas
was odd being out in the backyard without Marley, the Labrador retrie
who for 13 years made it his business to be tight by my side for every
cursion out the door, whether to pick a tomato, pull a weed, or fetch
mail. And now here I was alone, digging him this hole.

"There will never be another dog like Marley," my father said whc
told him the news that I finally had to put the old guy down. It wa
close to a compliment as our pet ever received.

No one ever called him a great dog—or even a good dog. He wa
wild as a banshee and as strong as a bull. He crashed joyously through
with gusto most often associated with natural disasters.

He's the only dog I've ever known to get expelled from obedie
school.

Marley was a chewer of couches, a slasher of screens, a slinger of dr
a tipper of trash cans. He was so big he could eat off the kitchen t:
with all four paws planted on the floor—and did so whenever we wer
looking.

Marley shredded more mattresses and dug through more drywall tha
care to remember, almost always out of sheer terror brought on by
mortal enemy, thunder.

Cute but Dumb

Marley was a majestic animal, nearly 100 pounds of quivering mu
wrapped in a luxurious fur coat the color of straw. As for brains, let

say he chased his tail till the day he died, apparently convinced he was
the verge of a major canine breakthrough.

That tail could clear a coffee table in one swipe. We lost track of things
swallowed, including my wife's gold necklace, which we eventually re-
ered, shinier than ever. We took him with us once to a chi-chi outdoor
and tied him to the heavy wrought-iron table. Big mistake. Marley
ted a cute poodle and off he bounded, table in tow.

But his heart was pure.

When I brought my wife home from the doctor after our first preg-
cy ended in miscarriage, that wild beast gently rested his blocky
d in her lap and whimpered. And when babies finally arrived, he
ehow understood they were something special and let them climb
over him, tugging his ears and pulling out little fistfuls of fur. One
when a stranger tried to hold one of the children, our jolly giant
wed a ferocity we never imagined was inside him.

As the years passed, Marley mellowed, and sleeping became his fa-
ite pastime. By the end, his hearing was shot, his teeth were gone,
hips so riddled with arthritis he barely could stand. Despite the
rmities, he greeted each day with the mischievous glee that was
hallmark. Just days before his death, I caught him with his head
k in the garbage pail.

Life Lessons Learned

erson can learn a lot from a dog, even a loopy one like ours.
Marley taught me about living each day with unbridled exuberance
joy, about seizing the moment and following your heart. He taught
to appreciate the simple things—a walk in the woods, a fresh snowfall,
p in a shaft of winter sunlight. And as he grew old and achy, he taught
about optimism in the face of adversity.

Mostly, he taught me about friendship and selflessness and, above all
, unwavering loyalty.

When his time came last week, I knelt beside him on the floor of
animal hospital, rubbing his gray snout as the veterinarian discussed
mation with me. No, I told her, I would be taking him home with me

The next morning, our family would stand over the hole I had
and say goodbye. The kids would tuck drawings in beside him. My w
would speak for us all when she'd say: "God, I'm going to miss that
dumb lug."

But now I had a few minutes with him before the doctor returne
thought back over his 13 years—the destroyed furniture and goofy ant
the sloppy kisses and utter devotion. All in all, not a bad run.

I didn't want him to leave this world believing all his bad press. I res
my forehead against his and said: "Marley, you are a great dog."

January 13, 20

They're Bad, and We Love 'Em Still

Man, and I thought my dog was bad.

Ever since I penned a farewell to my companion of 13 years, Ma
the neurotic and incorrigible Labrador retriever, my e-mail inbox has
sembled a TV talk show episode: "Bad Dogs—and the Humans W
Love Them!"

In the week since I wrote about Marley's death, I have heard from s
eral hundred pet owners. They offered condolences (thanks, everyo
But mostly they wanted to dispute the accuracy of my report.

Now I know I erred when I characterized Marley as the plan
worst-behaved creature. The typical response went something like, "Y
dog could not have been the worst because MY dog is the worst." And
prove the point, they supplied detailed accounts of shredded couch
raided cupboards, and sneak slobber attacks.

Oddly enough, nearly all the tales involved large retrievers, just
Marley.

Take it away, Sandy Chanoff of Abington Township: "Alex was what we
called a 'high spirited Lab' with a little attention deficit disorder. He ate almost all of my leather shoes, pocketbooks, and even the carpet. He would
greet us at the door with something in his mouth all the time, and would
jump all around like he hadn't seen us in years. He knocked everything off
the coffee table with his tail. By the way, we were also thrown out of obedience school." You too, huh?

Diploma Envy

Gracie, a golden retriever owned by Lynne Major and Lynn Lampman of
Drexel Hill, actually managed to graduate—and was so excited she
promptly jumped up and pulverized her diploma. Said Major: "She is loving and a little crazy at the same time."

Lois Finegan of Upper Darby said my manic mutt had nothing on her
separation-anxiety-challenged Lab, Gypsy. "She was a holy terror in her
eating curtains and their rods, doors, rugs, plants, and even a jalousie
window."

Others reported their dogs gobbling down beach towels, sponges, kitty
litter, spare change, even a diamond ring (which definitely trumps Marley's taste for gold necklaces).

Mike Casey of Pottstown beat them all. He said his late dog, Jason, a
retriever-Irish setter mix, once downed a five-foot vacuum cleaner hose,
coiled reinforcing wire and all—without so much as a burp.

Alyssa Burke of West Goshen feared the worst after her dog, Mo (yes,
another highly intelligent Lab!), decided to exit the house by crashing
through a second-story window. Mo survived the fall just fine, apparently
quite delighted by his newly forged egress. "He landed on a shrub, which
broke his fall," Burke explained.

Nancy Williams clipped my column on Marley because it reminded
her of her own irrepressible retriever, Gracie. She writes: "I left the article
on the kitchen table and turned to put away the scissors. When I turned
back, sure enough, Gracie had eaten the column."

I'll take that as a compliment.

Knee-Deep in Concrete

Rene Wick of Havertown owns "a lunk-headed yellow Lab nan Clancy," who decided to make a lasting impression on the next-d neighbors by visiting their newly poured foundation. "Clancy jum the fence and went straight into the still-wet concrete up to his kne Wick wrote.

And then came Haydon, the brawny—not to be confused w brainy—Lab that once swallowed a tube of Super Glue. "His fir hour, however," owner Carolyn Etherington of Jamison recounted, " when he tore the frame out of the garage door after I had foolis attached his leash to it." She adds, "In those days, we had the veterinar on speed dial."

Tim Manning of Yardley thought he had outfoxed his yellow I Ralph, by stowing a chocolate centerpiece safely on top of the refrig tor. "Ralph figured out how to open a drawer on the linen cabinet nex the refrigerator and use it as a ladder," Manning wrote. "We could tell cause the drawer's contents were all over the floor, and the chocolate devoured right there on top of the fridge."

All of which raises the question that any sane person must be askin; pets are this much of a pain, why does anyone keep them?

As Sharon Durivage of Yardley put it: "They give their love and loy freely and always forgive us for our bad days and cranky moods."

September 21, 2004

Shelter in Media Mocks Its Mission

o said it's a dog's life?

or the dogs—and cats—at the Delaware County SPCA, life is any-
g but.

s *The Inquirer*'s Barbara Boyer has illustrated in a series of articles, the
ate, nonprofit animal shelter in Media makes a mockery of its name—
Society for the Prevention of Cruelty to Animals.

)oes an organization dedicated to animals prevent cruelty by cram-
g dogs and cats into crowded, unsanitary conditions?

y allowing contagious diseases to run rampant through the facility?
blithely adopting desperately sick animals out to unsuspecting families
 then face either mountainous veterinarian bills or the heartbreak of
ing down the animal—or both?

)oes it prevent cruelty by sitting on a $7.6 million nest egg while re-
ig to provide a modicum of veterinary care for its animals? By having
terinarian on premises just two hours a week? Two hours for a facility
last year handled nearly 3,000 dogs?

' this is where cruelty is prevented, I'd hate to see the torture chamber.
Je humans expect certain minimum standards for our four-legged
panions: safe, sanitary conditions, proper nutrition, clean drinking wa-
compassionate care, adequate medical attention.

's not rocket science, and yet the shelter's 13-member board appears
less on so many fronts, incapable of getting even the basics right.

Goodwill Gone Bad

negligence is not malicious. It's benign in nature, good intentions
whelmed by poor decisions—or no decisions at all.

irt of the problem seems to be the board's inability to wisely tap its

$7.6 million endowment. Even conservatively invested with a 4 per
return, the investment would yield more than $300,000 a year in inco
at a 6 percent return, the shelter has $456,000 a year to play with. Yet
board members act like misers.

Nearly $8 million in the bank, and they can't afford $80,000 a yea
a full-time veterinarian? Sorry, but that dog won't hunt.

"The board of directors just sits on the money," dog-rescue volur
Arthur Herring the third of Montgomeryville told Boyer in frustra
"It's like a power trip for them."

Meanwhile, sick animals continue to go out to homes. Healthy ani
continue to get infected. And the pathetic cycle continues.

Boyer has heard from people who adopted dogs and cats from
Delaware County shelter only to discover they were desperately
One woman took home a cat dying from the highly contagious fe
HIV. Another adopted a German shepherd that spread a respira
infection to the family's other dog. Yet another took home a pit
mix, not knowing it was suffering from a highly contagious virus
internal bleeding. The dog required surgery, which cost the
owner $2,200.

Redefining "Humane"

A Collingdale woman took home a dog suffering from kennel co
worms, and malnourishment. "I could count every rib on her body,"
owner told Boyer.

That's what one might expect from a back-alley puppy mill, not fro
well-meaning group with the words "prevention of cruelty" in its titl

Volunteers have quit in disgust. Visiting veterinarians have compla
about the conditions. The state vows to investigate. And yet the board
in its heels, stubbornly defending its incompetence and clinging t
miserable Typhoid Mary methods.

When one former SPCA board member, Joseph P. Boyle, pushe

prove conditions at the shelter, he was forced off the board. Boyle told
e *Inquirer* that sick but treatable dogs were often euthanized because
ith was cheaper than medicine.

What is going on here?

Some animal advocates have begun a petition drive to recall all 13
mbers of the shelter's board, and that is a good thing. Perhaps a com-
te change in leadership is what is needed to get this sorry excuse for an
mal shelter back on track.

In the meantime, the existing board members need to tape reminders
their foreheads that read: "It's about preventing cruelty, stupid."

June 6, 2005

Animal Lovers? No, Just Bullies

e far upper reaches of Bucks County still hold the vestiges of an earlier,
ipler time.

Cows graze in pastures; tractors rumble along country lanes; open
mland, thousands of acres of it, stretches to the horizon, a quilt-work of
wns and greens and golds.

It is a place where silos still outnumber cell-phone towers, and where
ne farmhouses are actually still occupied by farmers with John Deeres,
investment bankers with BMWs.

A most unlikely scene for a brazen terrorist attack.

But it was here amid the pastoral tranquility of rural life in Richland
vnship, where the terrorists struck.

Not al-Qaeda or suicide bombers, but animal-rights activists.

Their cause: to keep animals from being used for medical research.

The innocent victims of their carnage: plants. Specifically, Chinese
nies, many of them rare and expensive, all of them ethereally beautiful.

pull my car off Route 212 into the flower farm known as Peony

Land, and the first thing I notice are the endless rows of blooming shru
Their fragrance fills the air; their vivid colors dab the fields like oil pai
from an artist's palette.

A Rich Irony

The next thing I notice are the obscenities scrawled in spray paint acr
the farm's barn. "[Very bad word] with primates, and get [very bad wo
by us," it states.

The vandals used the acronym ALF—Animal Liberation Front.

The intended recipients are Peony Land owner Michael Hsu and
parents, Chao and Susan Hsu, who had planned to build a kennel on
47-acre property to house up to 500 monkeys for medical research.

The vandals poured paint stripper on two cars and spray-pain
several buildings on the property. But what broke the Hsus' hearts w
the plants. The vandals dumped and smashed hundreds of delic
high-end tree peonies in a greenhouse.

"I was in disbelief that people would do such a thing," Michael H
told me. "To spray-paint our buildings and write graffiti is one thing, b
. . these are plants. They have nothing to do with our application."

I'm sure the culprits who trashed Peony Land didn't intend it, but t
left behind rich irony—the wanton and indiscriminate destruction of
living species to save another. Kill a plant, save a primate. Fauna rar
flora apparently does not.

In someone's twisted mind, it all makes perfect sense.

Another irony: The primates the Hsus had planned to import would
a role in research that could someday cure deadly scourges such as A
and cancer. They could help in fight against bio-terror. Or as Hsu pu
they could help "to extend the lives and save the lives of millions of peop

Thuggish Tactics

For the extremists masquerading as animal lovers, that is not enou
even if the monkeys are treated humanely, as Hsu insists they would b

In an anonymous Web posting, a group claiming responsibility for the
ndalism at Peony Land used the favorite method of thugs, terrorists, and
llies everywhere—intimidation.

"Drop your plans for a primate prison, or we will make your life a
ing hell," the posting states. "If you continue to go forward with your
ns, we will destroy your business, and we will destroy your lives."

In what Hsu insists is an unfortunate coincidence, the family has
thdrawn its application to house monkeys on its farm. Their decision,
u said, has nothing to do with the threats, but simply because he realized
proposal would not meet township space requirements.

That may be so, but he and I both know that the criminals who
geted him are crowing victory right now.

Reasonable people can disagree on the use of animals in medical
periments. But there are legitimate forums for airing such differ-
ces. A free society gives us that gift.

There is a word for those who instead would sneak around under
ver of darkness and use anonymous postings to seed fear and intimida-
n: cowards. And with the Hsu family's sudden reversal, my fear is the
wards will only be emboldened.

November 22, 2005

In the Next Ring, a Stepford Terrier

ent Sunday immersed in a world that has gone totally, unapologetically
the dogs.

Believe me when I tell you fur was flying everywhere.

Not only was it flying, it was being combed, parted, clipped, teased,
w-dried, poofed, and puffed. The last time I witnessed this much van-
preening, I was walking past a beauty salon on the Main Line.

The occasion was the Kennel Club of Philadelphia Dog Shows, which
tched across two days and 15 rings in the Fort Washington Expo Cen-

ter over the weekend, drawing 2,700 purebred dogs of every imagina
shape and size, accompanied by their perfection-driven owners, who a
came in every imaginable shape and size.

Some 15,000 dog lovers streamed through the doors to ooh and a
over the super pooches, and it occurred to me that if the Miss Amer
contest could capture a fraction of this mojo, it wouldn't be going do
the drain.

In the staging area, the owners fretted over their pooches, whi
waited patiently for their turn before the judges. Many of these dogs I
a good part of their lives on the road, going from one show to the nex
watched as a spectator patted a husky on the head, and his hand
swooped with a comb to fluff the violated spot.

Racing to Nowhere

I knew I was in a special world all its own when I headed for the ba
room and found not only His and Her doors, but Human and Canine
cilities, too. The dogs actually got the better deal, enjoying spotless st
filled with sweet-smelling cedar shavings.

In the rings, the handlers lined up their unflinchingly behaved spe
mens and began prancing around in circles at a half-run under the k
eyes of the judges. Round and round they trotted, hurrying to
nowhere.

A surprising number of the handlers were young people, many in tl
early teens. They obviously had invested hundreds if not thousands
hours into working with their dogs. What was up with these ki
Shouldn't they have been home playing video games?

The dogs were something to behold. They stood in flawless formati
their noses just inches from the tails of the dogs in front of them. Not
of them made a move. No lunges, no butt-sniffing, no hopping in the
as if they had invisible springs on their paws. No attempts at intin
relations. No two-legged floor dances. It was like I was watchi
fur-clad robots that had been programmed by Miss Manners.

Who was the official sponsor of this show, anyway? Puppy Prozac?

As the unofficial chairman and spiritual leader of the Dysfunctional g Owners of America, I'll admit to a little professional jealousy. I ldn't help imagining how my own late and not-so-great Labrador iever, Marley, would have taken the competition by storm, starting stealing the tablecloth off the judges' table.

f the kennel club had a shredded-couch division, I'd have had a o-in national champion.

Optional Commands

e current Lab-in-residence at the Grogan house thinks "Come!" is a gestion she is happy to take under advisement and get back to us on. 's never met a rustling leaf that hasn't been worth barking herself rse over.

very dog has its strengths, and Gracie's unique gift is her eye-tongue rdination. This allows her to leap into the air and smash her snout our faces at the exact moment we are opening our mouths to speak, wing her to jam her tongue where no canine tongue was meant to We call her the Phantom Frencher.

And she's the good one.

guess I came to the show hoping to find some small ray of hope that n award-winning show dogs shared some common ground with my dience-school rejects.

scrutinized the contestants for any cracks in their glossy armor. 10n, I pleaded silently, just one flying drool-stringer. Nothing. They ted; they pranced; they posed, not missing a beat. I came across one dle, so still and perfectly coifed, I had to look twice to confirm it n't stuffed.

"That's just not right," I said.

As much as I envied the magnificent über-beasts, I knew that life for n, as for all of us, was full of trade-offs.

Good dogs win all the ribbons, it's true. But bad dogs have more fun.

January 31, 20

Marley & Me
The Whole Truth

In light of the scandal enveloping best-selling author James Frey, w
now admits his purportedly nonfiction memoir *A Million Little Pi*
is riddled with fabrications and exaggerations, the online accur
watchdog SmokingCanine.com has launched an investigation into
other memoir currently topping best-seller lists. We now bring you
shocking expose:

PHILADELPHIA—Credible evidence has surfaced that *Inqu*
columnist John Grogan might have greatly exaggerated the badness of
now-infamous Labrador retriever Marley.

In his memoir, *Marley & Me: Life and Love with the World's W
Dog*, Grogan portrays his now-deceased pet as incorrigible, neurotic,
mannered, flatulent and slobbering. But a SmokingCanine investigat
found scant evidence to support the unflattering depiction.

One former neighbor, Betty Barcalot, told SmokingCanine: "Ma
was a great dog. I once witnessed him dart into traffic to pu
Chihuahua to safety. But did that make the book?"

Added a former nanny: "Yes, there was a lot of damage to the ho
but you should ask Mr. Grogan about how it got there. Let me just say
incompetent homeowner with power tools can be a dangerous thing."

Ice Picks and Drool

Reports that Grogan may have used an ice pick to intentionally
his home's woodwork in an attempt to frame Marley could not
confirmed.

Even Grogan's wife, Jenny, has distanced herself from the book, say
"Honestly, if anyone had a drooling problem, it was my husband."

Grogan now admits the amount of saliva produced by the hound was
ggerated. "I swear, it seemed like gallons at the time," he said in a brief
erview.

Grogan's book claimed Marley "chased his tail till the day he died." But
ily veterinarian Andover Yorecash called the claim, "absurd . . . beyond
ghable." He added: "On the numerous occasions Marley was in to have
ousehold object extracted from his bowels, I never once saw him chase
tail."

At a dog park Marley was known to frequent, a Rottweiler who gave
name only as "Fritz" said the whole book is a gross exaggeration.
Speaking through an interpreter, he growled, "Never once did I see
rley sniff a poodle's butt. And even if he did, is that so wrong?"

Fritz added: "I knew Marley. Marley was a friend of mine. The
racter in this book is no Marley."

Dutchess, a corgi who was once romantically linked to the buff
rador, added: "Grogan makes a big deal out of Marley's nutty behavior,
he was nothing special. Hello! He's a male Lab. They all act like that."

SmokingCanine has learned that literally hundreds of Labrador
iever owners have come forward to dispute Grogan's "world's
rst dog" contention.

Window Jumpers

d one, "I know with certainty that Marley wasn't the worst. Did he
r jump out of a second-story window like my Bunky?"

Grogan admitted Marley only crashed through first-floor windows.

There are even as-yet-unsubstantiated rumors that Marley is not dead
ll but living in seclusion in a canine rest home in Boca Raton, Florida.
"I can't swear it's the same dog," said Rocco DeRawhyde, an aide at the
lity. "But our resident, 'Harley,' is a dead ringer for that dog on the
er. All I know is just before the book comes out, these two guys in
glasses drop him off with strict orders, 'No visitors, no media
rviews.'"

Attempts to locate "Harley" were unsuccessful.

Grogan refused to comment about allegations that his original title
the book was *My Marley, My Dream Dog*, and that he only changed
premise after his agent could not sell the manuscript, saying, "The wh
Lassie thing is SO last year."

Oprah Winfrey, who recently withdrew her endorsement of *A Mil*
Little Pieces, did not return calls seeking comment on this lat
controversy.

February 27, 20

Zoo Hysteria High as Elephant's Eye

It might be easy to write off as a nutty extremist Marianne Bessey, the
imal-rights activist who has been banned from the Philadelphia Zoo.

Easy, that is, until you look into the eyes of the giant, majestic beasts
so zealously—some might say hysterically—champions.

Until you look into the eyes of a captive elephant.

There is something there. Something more than docile existen
There is intelligence, fierce intelligence. No question about it. Even
zoo's own Web site notes the animal's innate smarts. Is it my imaginati
or is there also sadness in those eyes?

Sadness and Longing?

Bessey thinks there is, and she has become obsessed with helping the zo
four elephants find freedom—or at least a relative facsimile of it—
2,700-acre pachyderm sanctuary in Tennessee.

She has become a major burr under the saddle of the zoo's administ
tion, regularly visiting the elephants in their tight quarters at the z
videotaping them, freely sharing her opinion that elephants deserve be
than a quarter-acre exercise yard where visitors stand and gawk at the

"They're so intelligent and just so amazing," she said by phone Frid

"A Little Depressed"

sey, a lawyer, became smitten with elephants as a child. "But when I
them in circuses or zoos, I always felt there's something wrong here,"
said. "They always seemed a little off or depressed."

n 1996, she traveled to Zimbabwe to watch wild elephants in their
ive habitat and was stunned by how differently they behaved and
racted from confined animals.

And those smart, deep eyes, she insists, had different expressions. Not
at all.

he calls zoo elephants mere "shadows" of wild elephants.

ast year she began badgering zoo officials to release the four elephants
he sanctuary where they could live closer to how nature intended. So
the idea has gone nowhere.

he's particularly frustrated over the fate of Dulary, a 42-year-old fe-
e with an injury that has kept her inside a concrete barn since August.
It's like putting your child in a closet for the rest of their life," she said.

As her frustration grew, she posted a message earlier this month on
online chat room known as the Elephant Connection. In it, she
hed that Philadelphia Zoo Director Alexander L. "Pete" Hoskins
ht experience what it would be like to be "kept in a concrete
et for six months to hasten [his] demise."

My frustration just boiled over," she said.

Vhat she didn't know was that zoo officials were monitoring the chat
m (your donor dollars at work), and they filed a police complaint
nst her, apparently on the theory that her comments were not-
e-but-almost-sort-of a little like a death threat.

A Threat, but to What?

v, we can't have death-threatening eco-terrorists at a family attraction,
t? And so the activist was banned from zoo property.

emind me again who's acting with extreme hysteria?

Let's get real here. The threat the zoo is trying to contain is not to director's life but to its well-coifed public-relations image. Zoos friendly, family places where all the animals are happy all the time. Th is no room for loudmouths questioning whether the elephants might better off running free.

I like zoos. I like the Philadelphia Zoo in particular, so much so th have an annual membership. I like taking my kids there. But I have to when I reach the elephant enclosure, I see it, too. Those eyes.

Most of the animals seem content in their enclosures. But the elepha always leave me feeling just a little . . . sad. If they could talk, you kn what they would say. And it would not be how splendid life is standing a rectangle of dust so people can take their photographs.

Other major zoos have released their pachyderms to large sanctua where they now roam free.

Visit the zoo, look into those deep, knowing eyes. Then ask yours Isn't it time Philadelphia did the same?

July 7, 2(

Puppy Mills Not Always Obvious

The sign rose out of the cornfields as we drove down a narrow cour lane in far rural Berks County:

"Vegetables & puppies for sale."

This was the place. The place we had been looking for. Our longti Labrador retriever, Marley, had died a few months earlier, and the sile in our home had become deafening.

It was time for another dog.

We were responding to a small classified ad for puppies of mixed distinct lineage—a cross between two types of retrievers. After our wi hyperactive purebred Lab, the mix sounded like a good bet. The bree were old-time, traditional farmers who raised dogs on the side.

I pulled up to the old stone farmhouse where Jenny, our three
children, and I were greeted by six stunningly beautiful youngsters.
They were blond and blue-eyed, their skin burnished from working
the fields. The girls wore bonnets and calico dresses to their ankles.
The boys wore overalls and brimmed hats. All were barefoot. No
adults were in sight.

Jenny and I exchanged a smile. We both felt good about this place. A
small family farm out of yesteryear; the real thing. We liked the idea of
steering clear of commercial breeders, some of whom have reputations for
being motivated more by profit than love of animals.

A Sinking Feeling

We asked to see the puppies, and the oldest of the siblings, a girl about 16,
stepped forward and without a word led us toward a cacophony of barking. Near the barn we found a series of rickety runs filled with dogs of
every imaginable shape, size, and age. None looked like the progeny of
two pure-bred dogs.

Two of the cages were rigged with spinning wire treadmills, like giant
versions of the exercise wheels found in hamster cages, in which little
yapping dogs raced endlessly. At once the scene was comical and heartbreaking.

It instantly felt wrong.

We began absorbing more of the scene. The puppies were crowded
into a makeshift pen, and some looked lethargic with runny eyes and
noses. Excrement covered the ground so thick it was almost impossible
not to step in. The mother dogs slinked around the periphery of the
barnyard, looking worn out and exhausted, their teats hanging low.

It was becoming obvious this was not the idyllic rural breeder we had
imagined, and that these dogs were being bred and sold irresponsibly by
children without visible adult supervision. We asked if the parents were
available, but got no clear answer.

Still, we persevered. Anyone who has ever taken young children to

pick out a puppy knows how difficult it is to leave empty-handed. T
puppies, even the sickly ones, were undeniably cute, and the farm k
handed them out of the cage one at a time for my children to cuddle

"This one, Dad; can we get this one?" they shouted for each puppy.

Nervous Glances

Jenny and I exchanged nervous glances. We both knew we would not
leaving with one of these dogs.

I called the kids over to the car for a huddle. "We're going to ge
puppy very soon," I promised. "But this is not the right place." T
kids hung their heads but didn't protest. I think even they kn
something was amiss.

As darkness fell over the unlit farm, we excused ourselves and dr
away. A mile down the road, I pulled over and we all scraped dog dirt
our shoes.

It didn't occur to me that night, or for months afterward, that wl
we had stumbled on was a puppy mill. Not one of the factoryl
commercial enterprises Pennsylvania is so notorious for, but a pup
mill nonetheless. A place that cranks out living animals like widg
for profit and often passes along hereditary and health probler
Governor Rendell is taking steps to crack down on these operatio
and I applaud him for it.

Looking back on my experience two years later, I regret not do
more myself. I should have made a phone call, should have turned th
in. But these beautiful, simple children were not what I imagined
wanted to believe puppy-mill operators could be.

A puppy mill, I now know, can take many forms. Sometimes you do
even recognize it until it is too late.

Celebrity & Me

k what Marley has dragged in now. Best-sellerdom is an unexpected
rich blessing, but at times the author has a bone to pick.

know exactly when and where it happened—the moment I finally
red out that my quiet, contented, boring little life had changed in
erful ways and would not be changing back again anytime soon.

was 8:30 a.m. on January 13, and I was sitting in the greenroom at
CBS studios in New York, waiting to go on *The Early Show*. A
eup artist powdered my nose and fussed with my hair. A producer
d me with a microphone.

was there to talk about my book, *Marley & Me*, and its surprising vault
1 obscurity to the top of national best-seller lists.

Vaiting in the wings with me to appear in the same half hour of the
ning talk show were rapper/actress Queen Latifah, movie mogul
/ Bruckheimer, and two young women with hardly any clothes on
billed themselves as "the world's only twin belly dancers."

Only on morning television," host Harry Smith cracked to me mo-
ts before we went on the air. I just shook my head. The scene was
al, and I was smack in the middle of it, about to go live in front of
million viewers.

fter my interview, Smith leaned in close to me and, in an almost fa-
y way, said, "I don't think you fully realize it yet, but your life will
r be the same."

e knew what I was just beginning to understand. For better or worse,
new status as "best-selling author" would change everything, even as I
ed change with every fiber of my being.

felt a little like the ordinary working schmo who wins the lottery. No,
ch that. I was the ordinary working schmo who won the lottery—my

case, the lottery being the infinitesimally tiny chance of writing a first b[...]
that, for whatever mysterious combination of factors, takes off.

What began in my mind as a "little book"—the simple story of [...]
early years of my marriage and the joyously insane Labrador retriever t[...]
would change the family we became—is now in its thirtieth printi[...]
with just less than two million copies in print. It has been on the *New Y[...]
Times nonfiction hardcover best-seller list for 34 straight weeks, 16[...]
them at No. 1.

Part of me is ecstatic at this startling success. Part of me still can't q[...]
believe it. And part of me worries about what effect it will have on [...]
family, particularly my three children, and on my lifestyle, my career, [...]
friendships.

I catch myself wondering: How did I get on this roller coaster, [...]
how do I hold on?

The journey began on January 6, 2003, when I published a colum[...]
The Inquirer saying goodbye to my hopelessly hyperactive, incorrig[...]
Labrador retriever Marley, who for 13 years filled our home and lives [...]
riotous bedlam. He was a very bad boy yet with a heart as boundless [...]
summer sky, and I wanted to set the record straight after years of mal[...]
fun of his total lack of self-control.

That column brought a flood of responses from *Inquirer* readers[...]
sponses that were highly personal. It was then I knew I had quite a[...]
dentally tapped into something bigger, something seminal. Not a [...]
story. Not my story. But the story of the journey humans and ani[...]
make together, and how the two shape and affect each other and bec[...]
magically intertwined.

After a dozen rejections, I found an agent, Laurie Abkemeier, who [...]
the potential in my story and decided to take a chance on me. I began[...]
ing at 4:30 a.m. to write before leaving for work. Week by week, cha[...]
by chapter, the story spilled out like utterances from a hypnotized pat[...]
without hand-wringing or self-consciousness.

Very early in the process I realized I could not tell the tale of this [...]

-than-life dog without telling the tale of my wife, Jenny, and me and
life we were just beginning. The two stories were inseparable, one and
same.

The book flowed easily out of me partially because I was convinced no
e would ever see it. As the book progressed, my agent kept telling me I
s on to something, but I didn't quite believe her. I kept wondering:
io in their right mind would want to read 300 pages about my ho-
n life?

But when the manuscript was done, in fall 2004, the agent's instinct
ved more accurate than the author's. She called me back a few days af-
shopping it around to say she had six publishers interested in making
rs. We sold *Marley & Me* to the William Morrow Co., and it hit book-
es in mid-October 2005, debuting at No. 10 on the *Times* list.

My publisher's aggressive marketing and publicity campaign—it gave
iy thousands of early copies to reviewers, media types, and book-
ers—gave me the big push it needed out of the gate.

But by the holidays, I became aware that something else was at play.
rley's rise above the glut of holiday-released books was being fueled in
e part by that elusive gift—word-of-mouth buzz. Bookstore owners
e recommending my book to their customers, librarians to their pa-
is and, most important, readers to their friends and relatives.

Attendance at my book signings was growing exponentially, from 40 or
in the early weeks to as many as 400.

And people were beginning to show up with multiple copies of my
ik in their arms. At one appearance in Chester County just before
ristmas, I signed a copy for a woman who tracked me down the next
k to sign 25 more copies she had decided to give as gifts.

By the time I appeared on *The Early Show, Marley & Me* was No. 3 on
Times list. A few weeks later, I was sitting in *The Inquirer's* downtown
sroom when Mauro DiPreta, my editor at William Morrow, called, as
lid every Wednesday evening when the best-seller list was updated.
But this call was different; he was on a speaker phone surrounded by

my entire publishing team. "Are you sitting down?" he asked. "Beca╷
you just hit No. 1."

All I could say was, "Wow."

I was similarly speechless in late January when I learned—by c
phone as I attended an author's reception with my wife in Sou
Florida—that Fox 2000 Pictures had bought the film rights. I put ╷
hand over the phone and whispered, "You won't believe this; they want
make a movie about us."

Jenny, who had graciously agreed to let me trot out the most perso╷
details of her life in the book, just smiled nervously.

The routine of our life was changing dramatically. I was writing my
quirer column and fielding a growing list of media and public-appearan
requests. And I was beginning my next book-writing projects.

The irony of my success was not lost on me—or my family. I h
written a book celebrating the simple joys of life—and now there ╷
precious little room for those joys.

In early March, I took a leave from *The Inquirer* to go back on the r╷
promoting the book—Chicago, Seattle, Portland, San Francisco, Los A
geles, Jacksonville, New York, Washington. Jenny felt like a single pare╷
on phone calls home, I got the impression my kids were figuring out h╷
to get on without me around.

And when I was at home, a steady parade of media people arrived
our door for interviews and photographs. Most of them made me pro
of my profession. They were smart, talented, fair-minded, and gracious╷
few reminded me why reporters are not always liked or trusted.

In February, I was in Phoenix when I began receiving e-mails sayi╷
"Do you know Howard Stern's talking about you on his show?"

Oh no, I thought, this can't be good. Stern, with his bombastic a
bawdy antics, was the last person I would expect to click with my boo╷

But there he was on his satellite radio program for three straight d╷
telling the story of reading the conclusion of *Marley & Me* while o╷

s-country flight and weeping so openly a flight attendant asked if he
led help.

le told his listeners he planned to write me a letter telling me what
book meant to him. I thought he was just blowing smoke, but a week
, a four-page handwritten letter arrived from Stern, and it was—
ly. Sensitive and warm. I now know what I long suspected, that there
ore to people than they sometimes let on, and there can be more to
jock than just shock.

My favorite part of this white-knuckle ride has been the people I've
along the way. Some have been celebrities, such as Diane Sawyer,
 interviewed me on ABC's *Good Morning America*, and Anderson
per, who I met at a publishing party a week before his book knocked
 out of the No. 1 slot. Most have been ordinary readers, from as close
rdmore and as far away as Australia, many of whom now seem like
family friends.

hey have formed a sort of Marley fraternity, sharing their pho-
aphs and stories at marleyandme.com and making friends with one
her as they wait in line at signings. Some write me poems, some
rd goofy songs, some bake gourmet dog treats for our new Lab, Gra-
In Denver, 180 strangers sang "Happy Birthday" to me.

n amateur artist shipped me a beautiful framed portrait of Marley she
ted in oils, which I hung in my bedroom.

ach morning, I look at his likeness staring out at me and just smile at
bizarre thought that my slobbering, never-do-right hound has be-
e a household name, not just in the United States but, with Marley
 being published in 24 languages, around the world.

hen I was on leave from *The Inquirer*, many readers wrote to ask me
was gone for good. I have to admit, I thought about it. But I love
spapers, this one in particular. I love writing a column and, above all
I love the readers who follow and respond to my work.

fter my first column back, a slew of messages greeted me, like this:
 Grogan! Welcome back. Now get to work!"

Yep, there's no place like Philadelphia.

On the home front, best-sellerdom has been mostly an incomprehe ble blessing but, as with most things in life, not without its trade-offs.

My sons, 14 and 12, are like most teenagers in that they cr anonymity. The book has thrust them out of that comfortable invisi ity, and sometimes they struggle with the notoriety. Many of th classmates, and nearly all their teachers, have read the book. People s them at school events or the mall to ask about it, making them squ uncomfortably.

I can't protect them from that, but Jenny and I have decided to m no major lifestyle changes anytime soon. We plan to stay put. Our hou our home (although we might add that new kitchen we've long drear of), our neighbors, our friends, our local school system, our childr universe. Besides, I can't think of anyplace else I'd rather live.

I've always celebrated frugal simplicity. I am the guy who fixes bro appliances, washes my own car rather than fork over 10 bucks at the wash, and scouts garage sales for steals. The income from the book movie rights is something we had never dreamed of and something will take some getting used to.

I upgraded my car, paid off some debts, bought Jenny the piano had always wanted, and splurged on a nice family vacation to the Flo Keys. But mostly we want to invest for the future—and share some v those less fortunate. Who could have imagined that dumb lughead do ours would put all three of our children through college and give us a cure retirement nest egg? Good dog, Marley!

As far as my children are concerned, all the hubbub can end anyt now.

One night recently as I tucked my 9-year-old daughter in bed afte days on the road, she looked up at me and said without a trace of pity: "You know what, Dad? I'm kind of ready for you not to be on best-seller list anymore."

You are?" I asked.

So you'll stay home again."

winced just a little and promised her I'm getting better at saying no.
n I reminded her we were like surfers riding a dizzyingly giant wave.
It's a crazy ride, honey," I said, snugging the blanket around her. "But
1 enough we'll be back on shore."

July 17, 2006

A Trek to the North Pole,
for His One True Friend

netimes a dog is more than a pet.

t can be a joy in good times, a comfort in bad, an unquestioning
nd always. The special ones can change a person's life. A very few
ht just land you at the North Pole.

or Barry Greenberg, that dog was Kunitz.

'or 11 years, the powerful, intelligent Siberian husky was at
enberg's side through the ups and downs of life. Kunitz was there
ugh a divorce and through career changes. He was there as his
er started over and found love again.

'or much of Kunitz's life, Greenberg, who now resides in Quebec,
1 in Wilmington and worked in West Chester as a biotechnology re-
cher.

Greenberg had never been one to celebrate winter, but the snow-
ng animal of proud Arctic heritage changed that. Greenberg began
ng daily with him in Brandywine Creek State Park near his home
soon caught what he called his dog's "winter lust."

t didn't take long for the Alzheimer's disease researcher to begin
ming of what huskies live to do: pull heavy loads across frozen
scapes of white.

Greenberg took his first dogsledding expedition in north
Minnesota in 1996, when he was 40. Seven more trips would follow
and his second marriage would take place on the back of a dogslec
the middle of a frozen Minnesota landscape.

"Kunitz," he told me last week, "was my best friend for a very l
time, with me through some of life's great trials."

In 2002, while Greenberg was in Sweden at a conference, the call ca
from home in Wilmington that his beloved husky had suffered a seiz
and died. "I never had the chance to say goodbye," he said.

Greenberg spread some of Kunitz's ashes in the state park where
husky loved to romp. But he saved a small amount with a special dream
mind—to one day travel by dogsled to the top of the Earth and rel
them on that vast ice cap where huskies' spirits never die.

In April of this year, Greenberg's dream became a reality. He joi
an expedition led by his dogsledding mentor Paul Schurke, the vete
Arctic adventurer. The group flew to Norway, where it outfitted it
with dogs, sleds, and supplies. Then it flew to a Russian research ca
one degree from the North Pole. The group then flew by helicop
with the trained sled dogs, sleds, and supplies to a point about
miles from the pole and set out on an arduous 11-day passage. W
temperatures hovering well below zero degrees Fahrenheit the en
trip, the expedition braved strong winds, steep ice ridges, open wa
and treacherous soft ice.

At the end of each day, the group of nine, with four sleds and 32 d
slept in tents on the ice.

In his backpack, Greenberg carried Kunitz's leather collar and a sr
plastic vial of the dog's ashes. On the final day, April 25, he lashed
collar to the outside of his pack, and the tags jingled as he walked, giv
him an odd sense of peace, as if Kunitz were there walking beside hi

The group arrived at the North Pole at 6 p.m., and almost immedia
Greenberg set about the task for which he had come. He walked a
paces from his cohorts, dropped to his knee, and used a knife to break

on the container. Almost instantly, he said, a strong gust of wind car-
the fine ashes off.

"I'm keeping my promise to you, Kunitz," he whispered, "You were a
d boy. You always will be."

And then he thanked him. For the companionship and loyalty, the in-
ion and canine empathy. For the goofy way he howled along when-
r he heard people singing "Happy Birthday" but no other songs.

He thanked the dog for helping him find a new life and a new wife
for setting him on the path to the adventure of a lifetime.

n the subzero Arctic air, unanticipated tears welling in his eyes, he saw
l so clearly, the way an animal can enrich and deepen the human ex-
ience, often in mysterious and unexpected ways.

"Thank you, Kunitz," he said.

October 2, 2006

Alpha Bet: It'll Work on Lids, Too

A Household of Dysfunctional Dog Owners Heels to the Will of the Whisperer

en my wife, Jenny, told me the Dog Whisperer would be coming to
home to help us become better pet parents, I admit I rolled my eyes.
am a plenty fine pet parent. My pets run all over me, and I put up
h it. You got a problem with that?

Regardless, it seemed this whisperer guy was arriving a little too late.
After all, our famously bad-boy Labrador retriever, Marley, shredder of
ches and flinger of drool, had long ago departed for that great obedi-
e school in the sky. His replacement, a shy, sedate female named Gra-
is so good she is boring.

"Um, is there something he needs to whisper to me?" I asked.

Cesar Millan came to this country from Mexico and slowly built a r
utation for his ability to turn around even the most problematic and (
turbed dogs. Today, he hosts the popular television show *Dog Whispe*
on the National Geographic Channel, and his dog-behavior book, *Ce*
Way, is a best-seller.

His big message is that it's usually not the dogs that need attitude
justments, but their human handlers. Dogs, like a lot of humans, are na
ral-born followers, but they will only line up behind a strong, confid
leader. Think Roosevelt after Pearl Harbor or Giuliani after 9/11.

Millan's mission in life is to instill these elusive leadership qualities
dog owners. He calls it "calm assertiveness." True leaders, he argues, do
yell or shout or lose their cool; they calmly and quietly assert their will
others.

Not in our house. Our animals are under the impression they live i
democracy, and they have an equal vote.

One day after watching his show, Jenny had one of those "why n
moments and e-mailed Millan's producers. Of course, they loved the i
of America's best-known dog behaviorist taking on what may very v
now be its best-known dysfunctional-dog owners. (My parents would
so proud.) Or as they put it, "that Marley family."

Last week, Millan and his seven-person television crew arrived for th
second of two visits.

During the first visit in August, Millan observed that Gracie, while r
urally pretty well behaved, was adrift, trying to find her own way in
world without benefit of a clear pack leader.

"You have her trust and affection," he said, "but not her respect."

Hey, just like my children!

Within minutes, and without ever raising his hand or voice, he l
Gracie bowing to him in supplication. He spent most of his time train
us to exert alpha assertiveness. Our dog just looked at me as if to sa
you're the pack leader, I'm Madonna.

By the time Millan returned last week, Gracie seemed to treat us with respect. She came when we called her, and sat at the door awaiting permission before barging out. The Dog Whisperer was pleased.

The more Millan talked about surefire methods to control dogs, and to their respect, the more I kept thinking: Forget the dumb dog; I'm ng this out on the kids!

As parents, we can't put shock collars on our children and zap them ry time they misbehave, but what if we used some of the same tech-ues Millan uses on animals?

What if we applied these commonsense techniques of calm, assertive ership? What if we forgot about being our sons' and daughters' pals instead focused on being their . . . parents?

Over a beer at the end of the day, I only half-joked, "Will you come with us and be our Teen Whisperer?"

Millan laughed, then volunteered that he receives a steady stream of er and e-mails from parents requesting just that.

With his own sons, 12 and 7, he said he follows a similar philosophy. gives them lots of chores and exercise to burn off excess energy, and s not to inadvertently reward bad behavior—even when it's cute.

He thinks twice before issuing an edict. Once issued, there is no m for self-doubt. Kids, like dogs, have a radar for weakness and will loit it.

And as with dogs, he believes one firm, memorable correction is worth ousand idle threats. In other words, when you say no, you better mean nd follow through.

Dogs are easy to figure out; kids, especially your own, quite another ter. And yet, as Millan and his entourage pulled out of the driveway, I oddly empowered on both counts.

Gracie looked at me as if to say, "Good riddance! Now we can get k to normal." My three children seemed to be having the same ught.

I leveled my gaze on the dog, then on the kids, and practiced my look of quiet confidence. I could almost hear Cesar whisper: Believe yourself and they will believe, too.

"Not so fast," I said.

Skip the Gun, Try Four-Legged Security

When the kidnapper slipped into 8-year-old Laura Staples's bedroom that Sunday night in 1998, he failed to consider one important point.

The Stapleses' Hatboro home was armed with a powerful se weapon hardwired to prevent just such a crime. A weapon at once pot tially deadly but guaranteed to never accidentally harm a family mem

The weapon was not a handgun or assault rifle or howitzer. It di answer to the name of Glock or Colt or Ruger.

It answered to the name of Rocky. And it was 120 pounds of fir tuned, rippling-muscled Rhodesian ridgeback dog.

The intruder flashed a knife and cupped his hand over Laura's mo as her parents, Michael and Joan, slept in the next room. "She gave it best fight, but the creep got the upper hand and started down the st with her," her father recalled last week.

As the girl struggled helplessly against him, her foot knocked a pict off the wall.

The noise was not enough to rouse her parents, but it did awa Rocky, who had been sleeping on the third floor—where he wasn't s posed to be—with Laura's older sister, Megan.

The dog charged down the stairs, teeth bared, and lunged. "The guy tried to use Laura as a shield, but Rocky was too smart for that," M Staples recounted. "He bit the bastard wherever he could."

Irrefutable Evidence

e intruder dropped Laura and ran for the door. Rocky chased him
vn and clamped his powerful jaws over the man's forearm, leaving a
esome wound that forensic experts would later use to tie a suspect ar-
ed nearby to the crime.

3y now, Laura's screams filled the house, and her father ran downstairs
ndishing a loaded handgun he kept in the house for self-defense. The
man was already gone, and it was a good thing, Staples realized.

His adrenaline was pumping, heart pounding, temples throbbing.
eams filled the air. Confusion reigned. In mere seconds, from a dead
p, he was trying to process an aborted crime that could have shattered
family forever. Staples, an experienced hunter and shooting enthusiast,
in no shape to be making life-or-death decisions with a loaded
pon.

'I was out of body. I wasn't Mike Staples. I was Hulk Hogan suddenly.
ould have had no problem blowing someone's brains out," the father

To this day, it unnerves him to think what might have happened had
not Rocky, confronted the kidnapper on the stairs, he holding a gun,
bad guy holding Laura.

'Had I been in the mix with the gun, bad things could have hap-
ed," he said. "When you have a 120-pound dog charging down the
s at you, there are no hostage negotiations."

Eternally Grateful

ht years have passed since that horrible night. Frankie Burton, a con-
ed child molester, was convicted in the kidnapping attempt and sent
rison for 42 to 118 years. Laura is 16 now, a junior at Hatboro-Hor-
n High School, where she runs cross-country. With the help of years
herapy, the psychological wounds are slowly washing away.

Rocky, an incorrigible bad boy who more than once was brou
home in the backseat of a police car after breaking loose to romance
female canines of Hatboro, got steak dinners, a parade, and the 2
National Dog Hero Award, given by the Society for the Preventio
Cruelty to Animals Los Angeles.

More importantly, he earned his family's eternal gratitude.

Three years ago, veterinarians diagnosed cancer in Rocky. He diec
May 12, 2004, on the night before his ninth birthday. "The sense of lo
was unfathomable," Staples said. "This dog saved our family. There ar
words to express the emotion or the pain."

The Stapleses have a new bad-boy dog now. His name is Junior, an
can often be found sleeping at Laura's feet.

Staples is a sportsman who is comfortable around guns. But he th
his family's experience serves as a good lesson for anyone conside
buying a weapon for home protection.

"I've thought about the gun thing a lot," he said. "After the bad
I just locked mine up. Guns don't work in the house. A dog is re
the best thing. Which is why I tell everyone I know, don't get a g
get a dog."

Life

New Scribe: A Suburbanite Geek

y there. I'm the new guy. New to _The Inquirer_, sort of new to the area,
with a new column that will appear here three times a week, focusing
the Pennsylvania suburbs.

eah, I'm one of those geeky suburbanites. When all my cool friends
attending Center City art openings in their black Gap tees, I'm out
vling around my front lawn worrying about the dandelions.

nd yes, shame of shame, there's a minivan parked in my garage.

My kids are always throwing these ridiculous propositions at me. The
er day, the 9-year-old said: "Dad, if you won $10 million and could
y spend it in one store, what would it be?"

thought. And I thought. And the only place I could think of was . . .
me Depot. Pathetic.

ou want to know how I spent a recent weekend? Building a tree fort.
I'm terrified of heights. I'm 18 feet up in the air in a swaying—sway-
—tree. I'm trying to hammer nails while holding on with a white-
ckle death grip. The kids went inside hours ago. Why am I up here?
nd why not the _Bulletin_?

My bosses want me to introduce myself to you. What can I say? My
grew up in Philadelphia's Germantown section a block off Chelten
nue. He still talks about swimming in the Wissahickon Creek. When I
him I got this job, he said, "_The Inquirer_? Why not the _Bulletin_? That's
big-name paper in town."

Uh, Dad, how can I break this to you?

By the time I came along, we were in Detroit, which is kind of Philadelphia without the nice parts. I was born on 8 Mile Road, r where rapper Eminem's new movie was filmed. It would make a g story to tell you Em and I hung in the 'hood together, but age-wise closer to Chaucer. And by the time I was potty-trained, my life in 'burbs had begun.

Journalism jobs took me from Michigan to Ohio to Florida and, t years ago, to southeastern Pennsylvania where I was editor of a garde magazine. (You can call there only if you promise not to ask me at your crabgrass.)

The last few weeks I've been wandering around the region a Man, is this place old. The cemeteries are all filled with Revolutio War veterans. Of course, South Florida, where I spent 12 years, si them as a newspaper columnist, has plenty of Revolutionary War too; the difference is, they're still driving.

This whole place is like a Smithsonian exhibit. Is there anywl George Washington didn't sleep?

I was in New Hope the other night. As far as I can tell, the ne thing in New Hope is about 200 years old. If this is New Hope, wh the Old Hope? I guess that would be Bob.

I see the region's helpful developers are doing their part to make there's plenty of new, too. If Philadelphia is ever invaded, we can rest knowing we've fortified the perimeter with Wawas and T.G.I. Friday's

Everybody Loves William

But it's the historic stuff that has me smitten. I keep meeting pe who insist their homes were originally deeded three centuries ag William Penn. Either that or by Penn's old college roommate, Sir Fr Lautenberg. (There I go exaggerating again. Frank actually bunked v Lincoln.)

What is the big deal about William Penn, anyway?

nd why is everything named after him? I landed here, too—hauling
e goldfish, two frogs, and a heavily sedated Labrador retriever, no
—and I don't see anyone naming the waterfront Grogan's Landing.

listory is so plentiful around here, it's almost cheap. The auto-parts
e near my house is in an ancient farmhouse that in most places
ild be a museum. The corner tavern claims to be in its 267th year of
cinuous service—and, trust me, the bathrooms are still waiting for
r first cleaning.

can't wait to jump in on the local issues. There are some real doozies.
his whole listeria thing has me freaked out. I've got listeria hysteria.

he other day, after reading about the latest recall, I screamed at my
: "For God's sake! I gargle with that stuff every day!"

That's Listerine," she said. "Grogan, you're an idiot."

isterine, listeria, Liz Taylor. Whatever.

⌐ December 24, 2002

Spreading Cheer the Interfaith Way

w nights ago, I went in search of true Christmas spirit. Guess where
und it? On the second level of the King of Prussia Mall, right in
t of the J. C. Penney entrance.

found it at a counter lined with wrapping paper, ribbons, and little
sh ladies.

he women—and a couple of their husbands—cut, folded, tucked, and
d at a furious pace, turning mall purchases into Christmas gifts.

hey did it without pay for a holiday they don't celebrate. They did it
cheer and smiles, despite hours on their feet.

hey did it as a mitzvah—a good deed to the community. Not only
: they helping harried shoppers—most of them wrapping-impaired
like me—with each gift, they where helping those less fortunate.

As chief gift-wrapper Sandy Heitner put it: "Not one penny goe
any of us. All the money is donated to charity."

The shoppers happily fork over anywhere from $1 to $8 a
depending on size, for the service. Many toss in generous tips. (
man handed the women a $20 bill for a $6 wrap, and said, "Keep
change."

Even the tips are donated.

The money will go to local police officers for bulletproof vests, to
fighters for hoses, to local libraries, to senior centers, and to the Red C
A local ambulance squad will get a chunk. So will Upper Merion H
School and the homeless of Montgomery County.

A Pint-Size Dynamo

Heitner, a pint-size dynamo with bifocals perched on her nose, and
husband, Jerry, have been working on the annual wrapping project s
October, when they began putting out calls for volunteers. Acting u
the auspices of the Jewish service group B'nai B'rith, the couple hop
raise more then $10,000 by the time the booth closes tonight.

"It's just like a little store," she says. "It has to run smoothly. We
these last-minute customers who want their gifts wrapped."

And on my night there, the shoppers lined up with basketballs
lamps, mirrors and nightgowns, waiting for the volunteers to work
magic. As one who has been there, I could feel the shoppers' relief. A
named Milton looked at me and said simply, "Worth every penny."

Third-year volunteer wrapper Linda Halpern of Conshohocken
the hapless men amusing, especially the dad who, amid the luxury s
of King of Prussia, asked her, "So, where can I find the dollar store?"

Standing beside Halpern was Dan Gross, a retired orthopedic
geon from Chesterbrook, wrapping a gift with surgical precision—
no sutures. "I'll try anything," he said. And the free coffee donate
a food-court vender isn't bad, either, he said.

Intense Couple of Weeks

e mall donates the space for the wrapping counter, and an Allentown
npany provides discount paper, boxes, and bows. Each night after the
oth closes, the Heitners tally the day's take, restock the cupboards, then
on the phone to line up the next day's volunteers, not all of whom are
vish.

"It is a two and a half week period that is very intense," Sandy Heitner
d.

Why do they do it? Why fight the mall crowds each day to wrap gifts
strangers when they can be curled up in front of the fireplace back
ne in West Norriton?

erry Heitner said it was to remind those who celebrate Christmas that
ir Jewish neighbors "are positive, contributing members of the com-
nity." His wife said it is simply for the good feeling of doing good.

Volunteer Chele Leyva of Chesterbrook, talking as she spliced paper
ether to cover a giant karaoke machine, said there's something about
wrapping table that brings out the best in wrappers and shoppers
e.

'You have moments when you ask yourself, 'Why am I doing this?'
t, mostly, it's fun," she said. "It's the happy side of Christmas. People
just so glad you're doing this. They're not yelling at you for cutting
ine."

Actually, it's much more than the happy side. It's the real and meaning-
side. A side where people of different faiths come together in selfless
d cheer to help each other. It's a side we could all use a little more of.

Weather to Croon and Swoon Over

I have been waiting half my life for a white Christmas. On Wednesda
finally got one.

Bing Crosby, eat your heart out.

True, 12 of my last 15 years were spent in Florida, where the o
white stuff hitting the ground was coming from the drug couri
duffel bags.

But for years before moving to Florida, I saw no Christmas snow. A
after returning north to Pennsylvania three years ago, I still saw none. T
last Christmas here to have even a dusting was in 1998.

At dawn I awakened to the roar of stampeding hooves in the hallw
Either Rudolph and his team had taken a wrong turn or my kids were

"Daddy!" the 5-year-old shrieked. "Santa made it snow!"

"Great. Go back to bed."

As if that was going to happen.

She yanked open the blinds. Outside stretched a vast canvas of whit
Wow. I was awake.

Being older and wiser, I knew Santa played no role at all. The real
son was that two days earlier I had finally washed the salt off my
which pretty much guaranteed a major storm.

Different parts of the region got different amounts, anywhere fr
a dusting to a dumping. In my microclimate, up on suburbia's br
northern frontier, big wet flakes kept falling all day. By the time
smell of roasting turkey filled the house, seven inches had piled up
the deck.

Snow Driving Wimps

Everyone was bailing on holiday dinner plans. The roads were just

cherous. May I say that we've all become a bunch of winter-driving
mps. Back when I was a kid, a little blizzard never stopped anyone. We'd
 crank up the Model T and off we'd go, a shotgun in the back window
:ase we needed provisions along the way. Now, a hint of frost brings
fic to a screeching halt.

Not that I was complaining. When it comes to relatives and holidays,
 firmly in the "less is more" camp.

My bachelor brother managed to make it in from New Jersey, bearing
s of dirty laundry for our washing machine. We call him Uncle Buck.

As the snow piled up, my kids were so ecstatic they raced to the
nputer to play virtual video snowboarding.

"You guys, hello?" I said. "You can do the real thing outside, you
w."

No response. Not even a glimmer.

Hello? Can anyone hear me?"

Am I the only father in America who comes with a mute button?

Eventually, I got their attention and got them outside—after earning
 Ph.D. in snowsuit zipperology. The kids had fun playing the Let's
f Ice Down Dad's Shirt game.

The soggy snow was perfect for packing, and soon we were building a
 that could have stopped a Humvee. One by one, the kids retreated to
house for hot chocolate. Eventually it was just Uncle Buck and me.

grown men on their knees in the snow, working away to keep the
ie front safe from enemy snowball attack.

When was the last time we had played in the snow together? I'm
ty sure Lyndon Johnson was still president. I looked at my brother
ugh the falling snow and saw someone I had not seen for decades—
12-year-old boy I had once shared a bedroom with. There was only
 thing to do: Wind up and nail him with a snowball.

Surprise Dinner Guests

My neighbor Steve pulled up with his snowplow. He and his wife ɛ
kids were supposed to be driving to Lower Bucks for Christmas dinne
the in-laws'. Not in this, they decided.

We had a turkey and no one to eat with. They had wine and no one
toast with. Besides, the guy had just plowed my driveway.

So dinner it was, two families thrown together by the whimsy c
winter storm that happened to arrive on a day we call Christmas.

I whipped up my nearly famous gravy. My wife mashed a few e
potatoes. Uncle Buck spiked the eggnog. And we had an improm
party. No expectations, no baggage, no stress.

After dinner, the kids played in the basement while the adults asse
bled toys. Outside, the storm had stopped, ensconcing our little world
pure cocoon of white. Peace on Earth.

Who knows? Maybe my daughter was right. Maybe Santa did br
the snow—a simple gift of joy and tranquility to a rushed and cyn
world.

January 3, 2(

Boob Eyes Tube While Driving

It's 5:20 p.m. on a workday, and I am merging onto the Vine Street
pressway into a wall of traffic. In front of me, a Ford Escort that looks
an escapee from the salvage yard weaves like a bee.

A weaving car in Philly rush hour? Stop the presses! But this
catches my eye. The passenger compartment emanates an odd blue-g
glow, the kind of otherworldly radiance you might see coming fro
spaceship just before aliens emerge and ask to see your leader. (What?
mean, you've never seen this?)

The glow gets the best of my curiosity. I slip between two trac

er rigs and pull alongside. This is what I see: A man watching
vision.

Jot a passenger watching TV. The driver watching TV. As he merges
 traffic. At the height of rush hour.

arth to aliens: Beam him up, please.

he TV is not some miniature travel model. It's the real deal, the kind
 might have on your kitchen counter.

nd it's somehow wedged on the dashboard above the center
sole where it blocks the better part of the windshield.

Survivor: The Sequel

ny commuting adventures, I have seen a lot: drivers shaving, applying
eup, tying ties, reading novels, jotting notes, and, of course, gabbing
essly on cell phones. I've even seen motorists executing several of
e multitasking feats of skill simultaneously.

ut never before have I seen someone turn a car into a mobile multi-
, What? No Raisinets?

m dying to find out what could be such must-see TV that this
anding member of the commuting public would risk his life and
yone else's around him to watch.

ouldn't he wait till he was in safer surrounding—say, while disman-
 explosives back in his garage—to tune in? I pull beside him again
can almost see what's on the screen when—WHOA! Here he comes!
hit the brakes. The truck behind me hits the brakes. The 13,000
muters behind the truck hit their brakes. And over drifts Mr.
tubby. No blinker. No warning. No clue.

back off and follow at a safe distance, watching the glowing Escort
d and weave up the Schuylkill and onto the Blue Route. I finally
 him at Plymouth Meeting when he peels off on 276 East toward
 Jersey.

here is Tony Soprano when we need him?

never did find out what my pal was watching. But I'm pretty sure he

had his own private Ralph and Norton show unfolding right there in
driver's seat.

If he keeps this up, he's sure to get his very own show: *Do You War*
Be a Highway Smear?

Crime and Punishment

Later, I talk to State Police Trooper Chris Paris at the Belmont Barra
This can't be legal, can it?

Trooper Paris assures me that driving under the influence of reru
definitely not legal. Specifically, Title 75, section 4527 of the Pennsy
nia Vehicle Code prohibits any motor vehicle from having a televi
mounted "forward of the back of the driver's seat or otherwise visibl
the driver."

"If I saw that on the road, I'd pull him over and write him a ticl
Paris said. Yes!

And the fine? A whopping $25 ($100 with costs).

Well, it's the thought that counts.

Trooper Paris wants to stress that looking away for even a momer
let alone for a half-hour sitcom—can be deadly. And more of us, he
are looking away—to dial cell phones, to eat Big Macs, and, in my cas
try to figure out what the guy in the next car is watching.

"At 55 mph, you're traveling 80 feet per second. That's the physics (
And who drives 55 out there?"

No one I know. Anything else?

"Any task that takes away from the driving is a potentially dange
one."

OK, trooper, are you about done?

"You are your neighbor's keeper. By driving carelessly, not only do
hazard yourself, but you put everyone else at risk."

So is this guy a complete moron?

"I would say unwise."

Trooper, you're kinder than I am.

OK, Mr. Unwise, here's a tip: next time you hear the boob tube's siren
, do us all a favor. Pull over.

Ditch the Speedo, and Other Fla. Tips

ok! Up in the sky! What's that blotting out the sun? Is it a plane? Is it a
up? Is it a flock of jumbo-sized Canada geese?

No, it's just the annual migration of the Great Northern Pale-Bellied
owbirds as they flock from their home range in the Philadelphia region
he fabled winter thawing grounds of South Florida. Caw! Caw! Caw!

With the temperatures in the Northeast dancing into the single digits,
 southward stream of half-frozen pale-bellies has reached a frenzied
e.

The signs are everywhere: darkened houses, boarded pets, piled-up
l, empty offices. Have you tried to find long-term parking at the air-
t lately?

The featherless snowbirds are heading south en masse, some for a few
s, some till spring, and I only have one question: Will the last one out
se leave me his long johns?

Unlike most migratory birds, the Great Northern Pale-Bellied Snow-
l is not protected under federal law, which makes sense, I guess, con-
ering it's the only known avian to fly coach class wearing loud
hing.

spent 12 years living at ground zero of the annual invasion—Palm
ch County—observing the pale-bellies interact, often disastrously,
h the native species. I went to help.

Here's the first thing snowbirds need to know before taking flight:
ridians will smile as they take your money, but make no mistake,
y're laughing at you behind your back. Snowbird character assassina-

tion is a favorite pastime in the Sunshine State—and there's no limit.

The second thing snowbirds need to know is, balmy skies and w sand aside, it's a jungle down there. This is a place where the T-shirts r "Don't shoot; I live here!"

So I've put together these Snowbird Survival Tips to help my mi tory neighbors avoid harm and ridicule while thawing out:

Leave the Speedo at home. I know it looked buff on you b when you where training with Mark Spitz, but time marches on. Sn birds tend to follow the inverse rule: the larger the body, the smaller suit. Buck the trend and cover up.

Try not to fry. Too many snowbirds assume the vacation is a bo unless they return home sporting third-degree sunburn. The lobster l is a sure giveaway you're a Great Northern fly-in. Floridians spend y perfecting their skin cancer; don't try to catch up in a week.

Steer clear of seniors. South Florida's large elderly population lc harmless enough, but don't be fooled. I've witnessed seniors duke it over parking spaces. In November, a 74-year-old man died from a l injury after he was slugged during a scuffle in line for movie tickets. suspect: a 68-year-old.

Don't become roadkill. Along those same lines, my advice is to off the roads. You think Philly drivers are out of control? We're a bu of Mario Andrettis compared to Florida drivers, many of whom hav had a vision test since Grover Cleveland was president. I've seen dri plow their cars into swimming pools, store windows, fire hydrants, name it. Mr. Magoo lives—and he drives a Buick in Delray Beach.

Speak like a local. Boca Raton, where I used to live, is pretty higl itself (probably because it has more face-lifts per capita than any o place on earth). Pronounce the town wrong and you are marked for So repeat after me: Boca Ruh-TONE. Not ruh-tahhn. Not ruh-Ruh-tone. If you really want to impress the locals, simply say, "Bowh-l

Drop the fib. Don't call your long-lost relation in Fort Lauder

say, "I've really missed you, Cuz." He'll see right through it. All
ridians have had this scam pulled on them. If you want to show your
rida kin you love them, visit in August. If you want a free place to stay
February, try the homeless shelter.

Don't get lured by the early bird. That great Florida institution, the
y-bird special, offers really bad food at ungodly hours for unbelievably
prices. The locals avoid these joints like typhoid. If you want to blend
you should, too.

Now go have fun in the sun.

As for me, I'll be ice fishing.

February 4, 2003

9/11 Altered Our View of Tragedy

Saturday morning I was in a high school cafeteria with 200 other
ents from across Southeastern Pennsylvania, receiving judge train-
for a regional student competition.

About 9:30, a man with a cell phone in his hand broke in, whispered
nething to the speaker, and then announced in a loud voice, "The
ce shuttle *Columbia* apparently has just broken up over Texas."

At that moment, I realized just how much September 11, 2001, has
nged us.

Two hundred people in a room, and this is what we did: Collectively,
mentarily, reeled back. Sucked in a sharp, short breath. Blinked hard.

A few gasped. One man in back asked for the information to be
eated. Another asked how many were aboard. A woman said, "Oh
God."

And that was it. We returned to our meeting as if nothing had
pened. Our collective shock and grief lasted all of 90 seconds.

Flash back 17 years and four days. January 28, 1986. I was a graduate

assistant at Ohio State University, teaching editing to a classroom full
second-year journalism students.

The door opened and a young woman from the student newspa
across the hall burst in, visibly shaken. "The space shuttle just explode
she blurted out.

The television went on, the now-famous images of those errant wl
plumes in the blue Atlantic sky playing over and over. Hands cove
mouths, eyes welled with tears, faces turned ashen. We stood frozen
hours, and our lives remained in lockdown for days as the nation ree
with shock and grief.

A Changed Landscape

Sitting with those other parents Saturday, the sense of *déjà vu* was pal
ble. And yet, something was jarringly different.

I was surprised—and slightly appalled—at how quickly we proces
the tragedy, compartmentalized it, and moved on.

What had taken us weeks to work through after *Challenger* took
less than two minutes. Not another word was spoken about it for the
of the morning. Speakers got up and sat down, presentations were ma
handouts distributed, questions asked.

It was as if *Columbia* had not really been lost. As if what had been
scribed to us was just a scene from a reality TV show. Real but not re
real.

Our ambivalence surprised but did not shock me. In the wake of 9/
the explosion of a space shuttle by no nefarious design was tra
certainly, but somehow less so than what we all now know is possi

I'm ashamed to admit that almost instantly I worked the numb
Seven lost. Seven lives, seven of our best and brightest. Heroes, gone i
flash. Horribly sad. And yet.

Seven is not 700. Or 7,000.

And yet.

A fatal mishap in the netherworld of Earth's outer atmosphere in a
rsuit as inherently risky as space travel is not terrorists striking ordinary
nericans as they go about the routines of their daily lives.

A Scale of Tragedy

d yet.

Death by nature's fury is not death by the hand of human hatred.

On the post–9/11 national-tragedy scale, this one, mercifully, fell
newhere less than a 10. That is not to minimize the loss, searing and
ofound, but rather to acknowledge the context.

We have changed. Our nation has changed. We are tougher now,
rder. Our hearts are no less big, but the innocence—that optimism and
nd belief in goodness we Americans are so famous for—is tempered.

We have been reminded—in horrible ways—that this world is a
ngerous, unpredictable place, and death can come at anytime to anyone.

On Saturday night as I watched the *Columbia* tragedy unfold on
NN, an announcer broke in with yet another reminder of life's
gility: Seven high school students, children not unlike yours or mine,
re buried by an avalanche in British Columbia. Seven more bright
rs extinguished.

I reeled back. Sucked in a sharp, short breath. Blinked hard. Then
oved on.

February 10, 2003

Her Shop Corners Market on Dignity

1 the matter of breast cancer, Marguerite Spina tells her customers, "I've
en there, done that."

Thirteen years ago, she was a West Chester wife, a mom, an auto insur-
ce claims adjuster chugging happily through life.

Then she found the lump. "That's what got the ball rolling," she says rolled her out of an ordinary life and into a place no one wants to enter a world of doctors and hospitals, chemotherapy, and surgery.

Before it was over, she lost her hair. She lost her left breast. And wh it was time to pick up the pieces and carry on, she nearly lost her dign as well.

That's the part that sticks with her all these years later—the humili ing ordeal of having to find a wig to cover her bald head and a silico breast form to fill the empty spot beneath her blouse. The sales cle were uncomfortable with her, which made her uncomfortable w herself.

One day she found herself alone in a storage room at a pharmacy, f ing a wall full of boxes. It was up to her to sort through them to find artificial breast that would fit her.

She decided right then that this was not right. And she began to dre of a store that specialized in just one thing: helping women navigate t frightful world of breast cancer with their dignity intact.

A Better Place to Go

"Women needed a better place to go where they wouldn't be treat like second-class citizens," she says.

Now a ruddy-cheeked, 58-year-old grandmother, Spina has realiz her dream. She owns the Yellow Daffodils Wig Salon & Post Mastector Boutique at 961 Downingtown Pike. With a name like that, you can it doesn't get many walk-ins.

Her customers arrive by word of mouth from doctors and otl breast-cancer survivors. They come from all around. One woman drc all the way from Long Beach Island, New Jersey.

The shop is in a converted farmhouse between West Chester a Downingtown. Open the door and it's like stumbling into someon family room, complete with wicker furniture and fresh flowers.

Four of the seven women who work there are cancer survivors
mselves.

"It's not a job requirement," Spina says. "It just worked out that way."

The women try to keep the mood light and upbeat as they fit cus-
ners with wigs, hats, undergarments, and artificial breasts. "I've had
ple say, 'This is the first time I've laughed since this all began,'" Spina
s.

But it can be a bleak business.

Her customers have been as young as 12. Just last month, a 17-year-
l with flowing hair was in to buy a wig in anticipation of her
motherapy. Most of the women are in their 40s and 50s.

"You have a lot of women come in here who you know aren't going
make it," she says.

Sadness and Satisfaction

ey are the ones you don't soon forget. A woman with a brain tumor
ne for a wig. She told Spina the doctors had given her two options:
e no treatment and live 90 days or undergo radiation and last six
nths.

"I never saw her again," Spina says.

And here at Yellow Daffodils, the bell can toll close to home. Kim
lgerwood beat cancer several years ago and spent the last four years
rking at the store, where she become a beloved member of the staff.

Then the cancer returned. "She fought it for a little over a year," Spina
s. "It just kept spreading."

Her friend died three weeks ago. She was 46 and left behind a husband
l two sons.

Spina and the other women who work here balance the sadness with
satisfaction of knowing they are helping women at a most vulnerable
e. There is no charge for the empathy, listening, and hugs.

"We've been in their shoes," she says. "It's kind of a buddy system."

Averaging just 10 customers a week, Spina doesn't make a lot money at this. "It pays the rent most months," she says.

But money is not why she is here.

She is here to stand as a beacon of hope for women navigating darkest passage of their lives. Her very presence beams a needed messa "We survived it, and so can you."

February 11, 20

Taking a Shot at Buying a Gun

"I want to buy a shotgun," I said.

The young man at the Wal-Mart sporting-goods counter didn't mi beat. "What did you have in mind?" he asked, unlocking the gun case.

His name was Bob, and he sported bleached hair and baggy, low-slu pants. I asked to see the cheapest shotgun he had. Bob pulled out a sing shot, 20-gauge New England brand with a price tag of $85.

Such a deal. I had come prepared to spend a few hundred.

Bob placed it in my hands. I didn't try to hide my ignorance. "How you load this thing?" I asked.

He showed me how to break open the barrel, slide in a shell, clic shut. "Then you're set to go," Bob said.

I had come to this Wal-Mart near Quakertown, in Upper Bu County, as a customer to see just how easy—and fast—it was to bu weapon.

What brought me here was the suicide of Richard Lee of Will Grove.

On February 2, police say, Lee, 25, walked into a Wal-Mart in Horsh and, after passing an instant background check, bought a 20-gauge sh gun. He then drove to a Wal-Mart in Warminster, where he bought sh

From there, he drove directly to Cavalier Telephone in Warmins

ch had laid him off, and began firing. The final round, police say, was
himself.

Blessedly, no one was present for the Sunday night rampage, and Lee
 the only casualty. But it doesn't take much imagination to picture
t could have been had he arrived during work hours.

No Hard Questions

d so on Friday I went to Wal-Mart to experience firsthand the safe-
rds that failed to save Richard Lee from himself. I sighted briefly down
 barrel then said, "OK, I'll take it." I had been at the counter for four
utes.

 was waiting for Bob to grill me about my inexperience and motives
wanting a cheap gun. Had I completed a gun-safety course? Did I have
 practice handling firearms?

nstead he asked me for two pieces of identification and gave me a fed-
 form that asked a series of yes/no questions intended to root out the
able and criminally inclined.

Had I ever been convicted of a felony? Ever been the subject of a re-
ning order? Any history of domestic abuse? Mental illness? Drunken
ing? Drug addiction?

f I had evil intent, did they really expect me to answer truthfully?

 handed Bob $2 for the background check and he phoned in my in-
nation to the state police's Pennsylvania Instant Check database.

en minutes later, he returned with a box and packed my shotgun
 it.

Does this mean I passed?" I asked.

Yep. No problem," Bob said.

 asked if I could buy shells for the shotgun, too. Bob apologized and
 store policy did not allow that.

We wouldn't want people to start shooting until they were safely out of
 store now, would we? If the ammunition restriction was meant as a de-

terrent, it wasn't much of one. There was a Kmart across the street that
ammunition.

On Second Thought

Bob rang up my sale, and I reached for my credit card. Once I paid, I
free to walk out with my new weapon.

But I didn't really want this weapon, and at Wal-Mart, as with o
gun shops I checked, all gun sales are final. No returns; no exchanges.

And so at the last second, with apologies to Bob for wasting his tin
pulled the plug on my little experiment and walked out of the st
empty-handed. The entire process had taken 27 minutes.

Just for kicks, I drove across Route 309, walked into Kmart and bou
a box of 25 Winchester Super-X game-load shells for $3.79. No ID
quired; no questions asked.

On the way home, I wasn't feeling particularly homicidal or suicida
deranged. But had I been—and had I not aborted my shotgun sale at
last moment—I would have been, in Bob's words, "set to go."

I later checked with the state police in Harrisburg, who confir
that Bob had properly done everything the law asks of him. Penn
vania requires no gun-safety training. No proof of competence.
cooling-off period. Not even an overnight delay. Just 27 minutes
two forms of ID.

That wasn't enough to stop Richard Lee. And it won't be enoug
stop the next Richard Lee, either.

February 21, 2

Tired of Sales Calls? Try Defense Tactics

Most of us agree that telemarketers are among the lower life forms on
planet, falling somewhere between mold and fungi. The only differen
they have better speed-dialing skills.

hey call at dinnertime, selling time-shares. On Sunday, selling credit
s. After a birth, selling college funds. After a death, selling crypts.
hey call. They call. They call.

overnment is trying to protect us, but, let's face it, the laws of a civi-
society don't mean much to lower life forms. Since Pennsylvania's
Not Call" law went into effect November 1, the state attorney gen-
has received more than 3,000 complaints from people who are still
ng pestered despite being on the no-calls registry.

ou might as well politely ask cockroaches to please not trespass into
cupboard. Sometimes you just need to reach for the Raid.

don't lightly advocate vigilantism, but in our house, we've taken the
nto our own hands.

eception is the key to the Grogan Telemarketing Defense System
S).

ne night, we were reading in bed when the phone rang. My wife lis-
d for a minute before saying in a heartbreaking voice, "I'm sorry, but
ny husband can't come to the phone. He passed away last night."

ne barely got the words out when—click—the telemarketer was on
ne next victim. I should have been thrilled, but I don't know. She
ded just a little too gleeful conjuring up my demise. Do I need to
orried?

The Name Game

any military operation, a successful TDS relies on early detection. My
and I have different last names. Anyone calling for Mrs. Grogan gets
rry, no one here by that name." Click.

angled names are another tip-off. If you don't want me hanging up
ou, don't call me   "Mr. Gorggins."

nother important weapon is the classic Three H Flanking Maneuver.
hree H was developed by my 87-year-old father, who spent the
10 years of retirement listening politely to every imaginable
e-on before deciding to fight back.

Three H (Hello, Hello, Hang-up) targets the soft underbelly of telemarketers' primary offensive weapon: the automatic speed dialer

These rapid-fire dialers are the telemarketing equivalent of howit. But they have one fatal flaw: A momentary delay before a live teler keter can come on the line.

Care to share your technique, Dad?

"You say, 'Hello? Hello?' And, if no one answers, hang up immediat

Personally, I'm a disciple of Secretary of State Colin Powell's doct of overwhelming force. This usually involves letting my 6-year-old dau ter answer the phone.

Telemarketer: "Is John Gorggins there?"

Colleen: "Santa brought me a Barbie Bake Oven for Christmas."

And she's off and running for the next 20 minutes, detailing her se to cupcake success while steadfastly refusing to hand over the phone.

She wears them down every time.

Could You Speak Up?

My other secret weapons are my two sons, the aspiring musicians. O learning trumpet, the other violin.

They like to practice at the same time. In the same room. In diffe keys. This fools our two dogs into thinking that a cat is being tort in the immediate vicinity, which sets them to barking ferociously.

Adults who have been in our house during rehearsal ask how stand it. But I just drink it in, grinning maniacally, one hand on phone, daring a telemarketer to call.

Go ahead, pal; make my day.

I'll admit, this tactic probably violates the Articles of the Geneva C ventions, but you do what you must.

Of course, blunt honesty works, too.

A couple of months ago, a seriously perky woman called to try to me a condo in "New York City's exciting theater district." I cut her o

"Reality check," I said. "I'm a guy with three kids, two dogs, three pet
ckens, and a mortgage that rivals the gross national product of
uania. My wife and I consider it a red-letter weekend if we can
ak out alone to the Wawa to buy milk. Then there's the college
ds. Do you know—"

Click.

And, gee, I was just getting started.

April 8, 2003

Burning the Flag as an Act of Love

e sun was sinking beneath the horizon, a chill in the air, when I led my
dren into the backyard to burn the American flag.

t was not an act of anger or rebellion or defiance. Far from it.

Our family's flag was a simple nylon affair, the kind you can pick up for
bucks at any hardware store. We would haul it out on Memorial Day
the Fourth of July and sometimes just for fun. Truth be told, it had
ome less patriotic symbol than garden accent. I liked the way it looked
ging off the back deck above the roses and daisies. My wife and I tried
emember to bring it in at night; but for long stretches, it stayed out
nd the clock, rain or shine.

Over the years, it faded, then frayed, and finally shredded. The last
e we had it out—in those dark days after September 11, 2001—a stiff
eze finished it off, ripping it into a series of sad ribbons. I simply
ed the tattered remains around the flagpole and propped it in a cor-
of the garage.

knew that was no way to treat the American flag, this proud symbol
reedom and sacrifice; and I promised myself to get around to disposing
t properly. But in a busy suburban life of yard work, home repairs, and
er matches, it became a low priority.

What It Stood For

As the weeks turned to months, the old, shredded flag gnawed at n
began to think about what it really stood for and how many Americ
had laid their lives at its feet these 200 years and more.

How many had died on September 11 simply for living beneath
banner. How many continue to fight and die in its name today.

In the face of this new, changed world, there was not much I could
but I could make right by that old flag.

So on a crisp, clear evening, with a firmament of stars awakening ab
as if to bear witness, I called my sons, ages 9 and 10, into the garage,
together we gently unclipped our old flag from its pole and folded
shredded remains as best we could into a tight triangle. A former
Scout, I had once been quite adept at folding the American flag. Bu
had been years since I had bothered. It took me a few tries to get it ri

I gave the folded flag to my older boy to carry, and we made our
to the back corner of the yard where the fire circle sits. The boys gathe
kindling from beneath the pines. Soon we had a small blaze that we
with walnut and maple branches until the flames jumped cheerfully
the night.

Seeing the glow, two neighbor boys walked over and joined us. I
them what we were about to do and explained why.

Moment of Silence

Without prompting, one of the boys asked, "Should we have a momen
silence?" And we all agreed that this would be a good idea. We st
there for a minute or more, the only sound the crackling of the burn
hardwood.

Children will sometimes surprise you. This night was one of th
times. Again without prompting, one of the boys placed his right h
over his heart and began: "I pledge allegiance to the flag . . ."

And the rest of us joined in. " . . . of the United States of America

"And to the Republic for which it stands . . .

"One nation under God . . .

"Indivisible . . .

"With liberty and justice for all."

I took the flag from my son's arms and nestled it into the burning
s. The flames immediately leapt as the nylon caught fire, and we
tched in silence as the Stars and Stripes curled up and disappeared
o ashes.

Tattered and worn, this humble flag of ours had graced our home in
od times and in very bad times, in joy and in deepest sorrow, in pride
l in anguish. It had seen babies arrive and Americans die. Now, how-
er belatedly, it was officially, properly retired.

We stood in a circle for a long time, the boys, normally rambunctious
l silly, saying nothing. The orange light of the fire shone on their sweet
es. As much as I tried not to, I found myself thinking about—and hop-
g against—the war they someday might be called to fight.

Eventually, my younger son spoke. "Dad, will we get another flag?"

"You bet," I said.

�a June 27, 2003

In Healing, Reminder of Life's Final Hurt

dozens of my colleagues hunkered down with American troops in the
qi desert, I was embedded in a life-and-death struggle of an entirely
ferent kind.

My post was a Bucks County nursing home, and the war I witnessed
er a six-week period was against that insidious enemy known as age.
Let me tell you, like all wars, this one is hell.

What brought me to the nursing home was not journalistic curios-
but medical necessity. Two herniated disks in my neck sent me in

search of a physical therapist. I found a good one who practiced
rented space in the nursing home's basement right beside a sm
beauty parlor where, each morning, old women caused a traffic jam
wheelchairs as they maneuvered to have their hair set.

Three mornings a week, I arrived for traction and exercise. Several
my fellow patients were just like me, in the words of the physical the
pist, "40-something guys who still think they're 20." Middle-age n
who stupidly overdid it and hurt themselves.

Yep, that would be me.

But we were the clear minority. Most of the therapist's patients w
residents from upstairs. Starting at 8:30 each morning, attendants in bri
floral smocks would begin arriving with them. Some came with car
some with walkers. Most arrived in wheelchairs.

They were stiff and weak and achy—and very old, in the final pages
the long books that are their lives. The physical therapist wasn't preter
ing to fix them. His job was simply to help them make it through e.
remaining day a little more comfortably.

Over the weeks, I got to know several of them and the world they
habit. It is a world most of us breeze past unnoticed as we go about
lives. A world of empty hours and countless days, not unpleasant
without future, where the only checkout is death.

There was Anna, a birdlike woman with a thin wisp of white hair, w
rolled in with her arm in a sling from a fall. The therapist and his 24-ye
old assistant tried to engage her, get her to do a few light exercises. S
would have nothing to do with it.

"Why am I here?" she asked.

"We're going to work on that arm," he said.

"Why can't I hear what you say?"

The therapist let the question slide, but she asked it again, this ti
more urgently. He knelt before her, his face close to hers, and said lou
but gently, "I think it's age-related, Anna."

There was chubby, cheery Sue, who each morning lay on a low tal

iggling to lift her hips a few inches into the air. One day, she smiled
etly at me and volunteered: "My mother always told me, 'Never get
.'" Then she paused, and the smile slipped from her lips. Somehow it
In't worked out that way.

Across the room was Doris, hooked to an oxygen tank and dressed im-
•bably in purple high heels. Her mission was to get out of her
eelchair without help. She rocked to build momentum. "One, two,
ee. Up you go," the assistant coached cheerfully. Doris tried and tried
in.

"I just can't do it," she said.

And, saddest of all, there was Violet, who by all appearances had given
Her job was to tug a rope through a pulley. But she just let the braided
'd slip from her lifeless hands.

The therapist admonished: "Come on, Violet. What's going on with
1? Show me you still have something in your body to work with."

But Violet was done. Checked out. She sat, gazing blankly ahead.

On my last day, I arrived to find the place nearly empty. All of my el-
·ly friends were missing, and for a brief, sudden second I was filled with
.ness. Had their time come? All at once?

But after a few minutes, in they wandered: Doris, still on her oxygen
t this time in more sensible shoes; Anna, her bruises turning yellow; al-
·ys cheerful Sue; rail-thin Ray. And poor Violet.

As they struggled with their routines, wincing and groaning, the
·ung assistant working the muscles in my neck, lowered her lips near
· ear, and whispered her confession.

"God, I hope I never get old."

Phones Driving Us to Distraction

Not long ago, I was a cell-phone virgin. I didn't own one and didn't w
one. I had a phone at work and a phone at home, and that was as in tou
with the world as I wanted to be.

My idea of getting wired was gulping a double espresso, not signi
my life away to Cingular.

In those B.C. (Before Cell) days, I made sport of ridiculing t
self-important chatterbox slaves who were convinced the wo
would stop—screech to a crashing halt—if they were out of tou
for one solitary second. I watched them droning on at restauran
malls, ballgames, picnics—and wondered what on earth they we
finding to jabber about.

Now I'm one of them, a cell-phone convert. And I wonder
more. How I ever got along without one of these things I'll nev
know. Equipped with my mobile communicator, I feel like Spock
a *Star Trek* episode.

But, like almost everyone else who owns a cell phone, I have a pro
lem. I can't resist using mine—to check voice mail, talk with my edito
return messages—as I hurtle down the expressway in a two-ton steel b
at frightening speeds.

As though Philadelphia's crowded roads don't have enough headacl
already, they've now been invaded by vast armies of mobile goofus ga
bers. To which I say: Reporting for duty, sir!

That Vision Thing

My favorite soldiers in this assault are the members of the bifocals briga
(of which I am a recent inductee). You see them swerving at you in traff
with one hand on the steering wheel, the other hand holding their c

nes out at full arm's length as they squint quizzically at the keypad,
ng to read the tiny numbers.

We chatty commuters are checking blind spots, passing, and merging
rush hour—all while yammering away about the minutiae of our
s.

f you see us coming, look out, because we won't be looking out for
t.

At least when we run each other off the road, we can dial 911 before
wreckage even comes to rest.

Do you think this is what AT&T had in mind when it told us to reach
and touch someone?

A first-ever study of driving habits by the University of North Carolina
nts a sobering picture of how distracted motorists have become. The
dy videotaped drivers in metro Philadelphia and in North Carolina
found that 30 percent talked on cell phones as they drove. The aver-
driver took 13 seconds to dial a cell phone. At 60 miles per hour, that
ans the car traveled nearly a quarter mile with the driver looking down
he phone. Oh my.

The study found that 40 percent of drivers read or write behind the
eel, usually while stopped. What is this, community college?

An additional 46 percentage groom themselves as they drive, and a
opping 71 percent bring new meaning to the term fast food, eating
drinking as they zoom along. Rule me guilty on that last count. If I
d any more selections to my front-seat buffet, I'll need a lunch-
gon license.

A Close Shave

my daily commutes, I've seen it all: Women applying makeup; men us-
; electric shavers; couples mashing.

I even know a guy who claims to play guitar while driving. You will
te that a guitar requires two hands to play, which leaves approximately
hands to steer with. In his own defense, my friend says he serenades

the dashboard only while cruising down lonely stretches of road. W
why didn't you say so, Elvis?

All this distraction comes at a cost to human safety. As *The Inqu*
Marian Uhlman reported last week, it is to blame for roughly a quarte
all car accidents, according to National Highway Traffic Safety Admi
tration estimates.

That's a lot of distraction.

I must confess, since getting my cell phone, I sometimes glance
mid-conversion and have no idea how I got where I am: One second
in Baltimore, the next I'm entering Chester. Hey, what happened
Delaware?

So, my fellow crazed commuters, whaddaya say? Shall we try regula
ourselves before the government kindly does it for us?

Here's a place to start: I promise not to call you from the road if y
promise not to call me.

August 25, 20

Hey, Ever Hear of an Ashtray?

Dear Drive-By Smoker:

You don't know me, but I know you.

I was driving behind you in rush hour on the Blue Route a couple
Fridays ago.

You remember the drive, don't you? Traffic was moving at a cra
through a steady rain.

As we inched along in a sea of red brake lights, I had plenty of time
watch you. It wasn't your driving that caught my eye. It was yo
cigarette.

There was something about the way you held it outside your wind
protected from the rain by your cupped hand. There was something ab

way you brought it into your new car interior just long enough to
v a quick inhale. Something about the way you cocked your head up
low the smoke back out the open window and the way you stretched
: arm out every half minute to flick the ashes as far as possible from
: new Toyota 4Runner.

could tell you didn't want to stink up your sweet ride. Couldn't
ie you; I wouldn't, either.

ut your smoking fastidiousness made me uneasy. I had a bad feeling
it where that cigarette butt was going to end up.

He's not," I wondered aloud, "going to toss that thing out the win-
, is he?"

Cars have ashtrays for a reason. Americans smoke more than 400 bil-
—yes, billion—cigarettes a year, according to the Department of
iculture, nearly all of them filtered.

A Long, Ugly Legacy

se cigarette filters may look like biodegradable cotton, but they are
ally made of stubborn plastic filaments that can take years, even
des, to break down.

very year, hundreds of millions of these butts are mindlessly flicked
car windows, off patios, over railings, into gardens and, of course, onto
hes where toddlers gravitate to them like candy.

Not only do they become semipermanent additions to the landscape,
the poisons they are designed to trap also slowly leach out and find
r way into streams and lakes.

Charming, huh?

o, you see, Drive-By Smoker, I was worried about that butt of
rs. One butt may seem like no big deal, but multiply it by 100 mil-
and you have an environmental hazard. What would *you* be? Part of
problem or part of the solution?

watched as you pulled the smoldering butt back into the car for one

long, last drag. The moment of truth had arrived. Would you snuff it
in your car's spotless ashtray? Or would you make the world your ash

I wanted to believe in you. Not all smokers are inconsiderate s
right? I've met smokers who are so conscientious they carry small n
canisters in their pockets to hold their butts until they reach a trash
But they're the exception.

Many smokers, it seems, have convinced themselves that a few bi
cigarette butts littering the roadsides of America are no big deal. Each
dividual butt is so small, it doesn't really count as littering, does it?

I particularly love the smokers who conscientiously use their asht
but then, once full, dump them in public parking lots. Pigs. Total pigs

Not a Bad Person

I caught your face in profile a couple of times. You looked like a p
decent sorta guy who works hard, pays his taxes, maybe coaches L
League. A guy who suffers through rush hour to get home to his fa
in the suburbs in time for dinner.

You looked like the kind of person who would not consider for a
ment tossing a soda can or bag of fast-food debris out your car windo

And yet here you were with a cigarette butt poised in your har
watched as you expertly balanced it between your thumb and forefi
and slowly exhaled your final puff.

And then, with a graceful flick, you sent that butt arcing through
dusk and onto the shoulder of the highway, where it sat in a puddl
rainwater.

On behalf of all of us who will live with this little testament to y
slovenly thoughtlessness for the next 25 years, I'd like to thank you.
behalf of the fish and birds and animals. On behalf of the plants and
and water. On behalf of all our children and grandchildren. Thank you
the gift that keeps on giving.

Letting Go of the One That Got Away

rets. Every life has them, some more than others. Lately, I have had
one: the home that got away.

saw it on my first day of house hunting in Southeastern Pennsylvania,
nbling serendipitously upon it as if led by divine compass. I took a
ng turn and then another, and soon I was hopelessly lost on a stripe-
country lane. I followed the lane down a steep hill and through a
d of hardwoods.

And there it was.

tanding close against the trees in a meadow that hadn't been mowed,
imestone walls glowing in the morning sun—an 1840s farmhouse. A
rious, lovely farmhouse with deep windowsills, a slate roof, and a
ch from which you could imagine the original owners waving
well as their sons trudged off to defend the Union.

t sat on five rolling acres with a spring and a view. And there was a
sale sign out front. Gulp!

This was the place my wife and I had dreamed of. The garden could go
e, the chicken coop there. Best of all, a tiny stone cottage, which I later
ned was the original homestead, still stood on the edge of the prop-
—a writing studio waiting to happen.

was soon back with my wife and a real estate agent. She pushed open
front door, and our hearts sank.

The Money Pit

ls were caved in. Floors scarred. Ceilings buckled. Loose wiring hung
n the rafters. The kitchen was missing in action. A hot plate and dirty
es on the toilet told us where the cooking now was done.

Suddenly I knew why the house was in our price range. Everywhere

we looked we saw work—and bills. The plumbing, the wiring, the pla
the chimney, the heating, the cellar all required overhauls. Tens of th
sands of dollars were needed just to make it habitable, and tens of th
sands more—and hundreds of hours of our time—if it were eve
reclaim its charm.

And still, after a brief ashen silence, my wife and I began plotting.

"This wall could come out," I said.

"The kitchen could go here," she said.

Our agent stood quietly. She had seen it all before. The young cou
with big dreams and the way these stone seductresses lured them
chewed them up, and spat them out, broke and broken.

Finally, she frowned and said: "You have three young children an
new job. In good conscience, I cannot let you buy this place." She kr
the score. We could barely afford the asking price, let alone the nee
renovations. And I wasn't exactly Bob Vila.

Still, we dithered. We agonized. We wrote up a five-year work plan
the end, we followed our agent's advice and bought a sensible, subur
two-story with maintenance-free vinyl siding and a new furnace.

And lived happily ever after. Well, almost. It was just our luck that
became close friends with the people next door to the old farmho
Every time we visited, we were reminded of our choice. For months,
house stood empty, and we felt only relief. We congratulated ourselves
not stumbling into that sorry quagmire.

A Vision Realized

But then a young couple bought the place and began doing everyth
we had dreamed of doing. They mowed down the weeds, raised a ba
dug a pond, erected a split-rail fence.

Then one day at dinner at our friends', we met them. And they invi
us over to see the inside. We could not believe it was the same hou
Walls had been moved, the plaster repaired and painted, the plank flo
refinished, a new kitchen installed.

We gushed about the wonderful job they had done. But I saw it be-
d my wife's smile, and she saw it behind mine. Inside, we were aching.
t was our house just as we had imagined it. But it wasn't ours. It was
one we let get away. Regrets.

wanted to begrudge this couple their trophy. Quite honestly, I wanted
ate them. But they were much too nice for that. I had to admit they
sessed what I did not: the energy, skill, creativity and, most important,
i in their vision to pull it off.

es, and the money, too.

Where I saw nothing but heartache, they saw limitless potential.

They deserve their trophy manor. And I'm learning to love my conso-
on prize, vinyl siding and all.

October 7, 2003

Haunting Glimpse at a Stranger's Life

month has passed, and still she haunts me.

from vastly different worlds, we came briefly together—a middle-
l, white man from the suburbs and a young black woman from the
ects.

We never even said our names.

was driving into the faded Western Pennsylvania steel city of John-
vn on assignment—and was lost.

exited the expressway to ask directions and found myself amid several
-slung brown buildings—a subsidized housing project. Young men
d about in groups, killing time. On a street corner near them, a wisp
girl stood alone.

he wore her hair in a short, stubby ponytail, and the wire-framed
ses perched on her nose gave her the look of a schoolgirl. I rolled
vn my window and asked how to get downtown.

She began to try to direct me, and then she stopped and looked at
sky as if trying to solve a riddle.

"You know what?" she said. "I've been standing here for an h
waiting for the bus, and if I don't get downtown in the next half ho
I'm sunk."

"Can I have a ride?"

Could she have a ride? In the seconds that ticked by before I
swered, I thought of a hundred reasons why, no, she could not.

We were strangers. She didn't know if she could trust me. I didn't kn
if I could trust her. She was just a kid. In 2003, young women do not
into cars with strange men, do they? And men of honorable intent d
allow them to, do they?

The Whiff of Impropriety

And there was the appearance. Older guy pulls up alongside m
younger woman on street corner; she leans in, then gets in. I could
see myself explaining it to the vice detail waiting around the corner.

Everything said no. And yet something about this young woman t
me she really needed this ride. "I could show you the way," she offere

I hesitated one last moment, then blurted out, "Sure. Hop in."

Before I could clear the junk off the front passenger seat, she slid i
the backseat. And I knew from her expression that this was a defensive move
the farthest seat from my reach.

"Late for work?" I asked as we drove off through the stares of the
young men. But there was no job.

She was 20 years old and the single mother of a 16-month-old dau
ter. She needed to get to the courthouse before it closed, she said, or
the baby's father would be going to jail for failing to pay child suppor

"I need to tell them he's a good man," she said. "He's a good dad."

A good dad leaves her to raise this child alone? She said putting hin
jail would solve nothing.

She told me she had grown up in Erie as a ward of the state, be

nced from one foster home to the next. The day she turned 18 was
day she struck out on her own with dreams of building a better life.

Flight to Nowhere

hy Johnstown?" I asked.

he shrugged. "Because it wasn't Erie," she answered.

oon she was pregnant. By 19, she was a mother, alone no more but
a no way to support herself and her child except for government assis-
e. How differently life might have turned out for her, I wondered, had
been dealt the basic hand every child deserves: a stable home and lov-
parents.

Vhat if someone had believed in her worth and let her know it? What
ht she be now?

A college student? An apprentice in a trade? A woman on the first
g of her career? Perhaps she would be something other than on pub-
ssistance facing an uphill battle to avoid repeating for her daughter the
e poverty and dependency she herself was born into.

pulled in front of the courthouse, and she opened the car door.

Thanks for the ride," she said.

s much as you can like someone after 20 minutes, I liked her. I
ted to tell her that it was not too late to reach for her dreams. She
20 years old with her whole life ahead of her. She could still make
ething better of it. I wanted to tell her she owed it to her daughter
ry.

Vhat I said instead was. "Good luck." And I meant it.

he smiled, then loped across the street and through the big court-
se doors with nine minutes to spare.

January 20, 2(

Let No Chip Put This Vow Asunder

I waited until the kids were on the school bus before I confronted wife by the coffeemaker and said: "Honey, I have a confession to make

She looked at me with that nervous grin she gets when bracing for worst.

"I cheated," I said. "I'm sorry."

"I can't believe this," she said.

It was true. I had violated our shared vow of carbohydrate celib and low-fat fidelity. I had strayed from our joint diet—straight into crunchy embrace of a bag of Doritos. I wish I could say I didn't er it, but I did. Each bite was pure bliss.

Believe me, I'm not proud of myself.

As my wife pointed out, we had a deal, struck during a calorie-cra vacation to Disney World over Christmas. "This is it," I said as we p ished off chocolate-covered ice cream bars outside Space Mount. "When we get home, we're going on a diet."

My cheapskate gene had finally trumped my chowhound gene. I eit had to drop 10 pounds and a couple of inches or replace my wardrob

Jenny is lanky by design. But she, too, has noticed that one of many charming aspects of rounding the halfway point to 90—al with those stylish Grandpa Walton bifocals and an utter inability to awake through the 11 o'clock news—is that calories no longer b themselves into oblivion as they once did.

Till Chips Do We Part

"I'm in," she said. And right then we exchanged our vows. We wo support and encourage each other, on good weigh-in days and bad fullness and in hunger, through cake cravings and linguine lusts.

Many of our friends were on low-carbohydrate diets, and, frankly, it
n't sound all that tough. You still got to eat all the good stuff like
k and ham. All you were cutting out were the things that went
und them—the rice and pasta and breads and sweets. How hard
ld that be?

New Year's Day came, and we launched our diet by dropping in on
friends Mike and Patti for an impromptu pizza-and-beer party.
ere's to our new low-carb diet!" I toasted.

The next day, we got another invitation for pizza and beer. "Tomorrow,
start for sure." I vowed. And we did.

Life knows no joy like opening the day with runny eggs without
st washed down with unsweetened coffee. My children taunted me
gnawing on huge, doughy bagels.

By dinner (a chicken breast with salad), I was so crazed for carbs I nearly
kled my son as he carried a bowl of macaroni to the table. That night
reamed of bread and butter.

By Day 3, I was fantasizing about being locked overnight in a bak-
. On Day 7, I looked out the window and saw plates of steaming
atoni floating by. On Day 9, I said to Jenny: "My wardrobe needs
dating, anyway."

And on Day 10, I spotted the Doritos.

Surrendering to Desire

e bag lay on top of the refrigerator, wantonly open, barely folded
r. O, be still my low-carb cheatin' heart!

I stepped closer. The bag's siren call filled my ears, seeming to say:
u know you want me." I knew I did. My arm, of its own volition,
ched up.

"Look away from the chips!" my dieting partner barked. Busted.

But it was only a matter of time. In my heart, I had already strayed. For
next couple of days I searched for excuses to walk past the refrigera-
, shooting furtive glances up at the little home-wrecker.

Jenny and I had each lost a few pounds. The diet was working. Bu
what cost? Was a life without bread and pie and chips and beer—d
mention no beer?—worth living?

And so, I did it. Late that night, when everyone was asleep, I lit i
the bag. Just one chip, I promised. Then it was two. Then three. Soc
lost count.

The next day, a few hours after my confession, my wife called m
work. "I just ate popcorn," she said. "With butter."

"Oh, that is so like a woman," I seethed. "One little lapse on your h
band's part and you're dragging home Orville Redenbacher."

Eventually, we worked things out. The joint diet is holding—t
thread. It may take counseling, but I think we're going to
through this.

And you know what? Our marriage will be stronger for it. Assumi
of course, a warm loaf of bread doesn't show up at the door anyti
soon.

February 23, 2C

He Helps Iraq's Children and America's Cause

Until a little more than a year ago, Thomas Murt was just anotl
suburban dad.

He coached youth sports for his three children's teams and tau;
catechism at St. David's Catholic Church in Willow Grove.

He was an Upper Moreland Township commissioner and made
living as an academic adviser at Pennsylvania State University's Abing
campus. Life was comfortable.

Then on January 24, 2003, the fax machine in his office rattled ou
slip of paper that would change everything.

Murt's Army Reserve unit was being sent to Iraq. Less than 24 ho

r, he was on a plane to Fort Drum, New York, and within weeks
nd himself on the ground in Saddam Hussein's volatile hometown of
krit. "He was gone before we really had a chance to say goodbye," his
fe, Maria, said.

It was there in the desert sands that this man's ordinary life took a turn for
e extraordinary. On his own, he has informally adopted hundreds of
poverished Iraqi children—and in so doing he is helping the United States
n its biggest battle of all, the battle for the trust of the Iraqi people.

Staff Sargent Murt, 43, who resigned his elected Upper Moreland post
nen he was deployed, was assigned to serve as a bodyguard and driver
 his company commander. He also provided security for civil-affairs
ssions into the countryside, which included the rebuilding of local
nools.

The frequent forays into remote villages gave him an up-close look at
nat life was like for thousands of ordinary Iraqis, nearly all of them living
 abject poverty. The children especially moved him. Most had no
noolbooks or pencils, nor even a sweater or single pair of socks to see
em through the cold winter.

Murt has always had a soft spot for children in need. His wife, who
s been managing the family home for more than a year now as a
ngle parent, remembers the couple's 1989 honeymoon to Grenada.
ithout telling her, Murt brought along two large suitcases filled with
othing and toys for children at a local orphanage.

"It's just always been part of him," she said.

Now in Iraq, Murt saw a whole new level of need. And he got an idea.
is coworkers and neighbors had been sending him boxes of toiletries
d gifts to share with his fellow soldiers.

He appreciated the outpouring but felt the generosity could be better
rected. So he sent e-mails to everyone he knew, with photos of the Iraqi
ildren he had befriended, asking them instead to send old clothing,
ys, costume jewelry, and school supplies.

"Many of the things we take for granted in the U.S. are great luxur[ies] here," he wrote.

From around Upper Moreland and Willow Grove and Hatboro, [the] community responded, and boxes of donated goods began to roll [in.] Dozens of boxes, shipped by domestic mail to Fort Drum, then abo[ard] military transport planes to Iraq, all addressed to Murt, "He was w[ell] known at the [base] mail room," his wife said.

His coworkers at Penn State Abington sent 35 boxes. Boy Scout Tro[op] 336 in Willow Grove collected 935 pounds of school supplies. At [St.] David's, Sister Rita, the principal, put out the call for children to sc[our] their toy chests.

Pete's Barber Shop in Hatboro got in on the act. So did ma[ny] neighbors. Annie Gleave, who works at the Hatboro post office a[nd] took a lead in organizing donations, said Murt's photos of shoeless Ir[aqi] children touched her. "It's made me see what's really important in lif[e]," she said.

And Murt said the community's outpouring, in turn, has touched t[he] Iraqi children and their families. Many now consider the Americans th[eir] friends.

"By working with the children and villagers, we have a gold[en] opportunity to teach them that we are not their enemy," wrote Mu[rt,] who hopes to be home in the next six to eight weeks and asks that [no] more donations be sent.

And isn't that where victory lies? One soldier, one community win[?]-ning over a country one child at a time.

Said Upper Moreland resident Kathy Rusch, who was involved in t[he] donation drive: "With Tom, this is not an unusual thing. This is how [he] lives his life. He is just one of those people who gives a damn."

March 11, 2004

TV Weather Is a Flurry of Hysteria

watched from my kitchen window yesterday morning as a few
wflakes drifted down, melting as they touched the pavement, a
ifying chill ran through me.

Not another one, I thought. Not another flashback to the winter
will live in infamy. No, it wasn't the season's weather that had me
ound. The weather was just fine, actually on the wimpy side for
nsylvania.

was the television news coverage of the weather that left me
king. This was the year of the hysterical "We all could die!"
ter-storm alert.

No matter how modest the dusting outside, you could turn on any of
local television stations and hear something that went like this:

Dramatic music plays; a video montage shows howling blizzard condi-
s, the likes of which have not been seen in this region for years.)

We interrupt this program for a special storm advisory.

Anchor Brent Blowdried: Well, folks, this is what all of us have been
ding. What just might be the storm of the century may be heading
way, bringing with it the possibility of death, destruction, mayhem,
indescribable heartbreak.

Co-anchor Brenda Bigteeth: That's right, Brent. This could be one
the record books. Our team coverage begins right now at the base
he Walt Whitman Bridge where reporter Bunny Snowsuit is stand-
by. Bunny, what can you tell us?

nowsuit: We now have confirmed sightings of at least seven—I
eat, seven—snowflakes sticking to the bridge behind me. And we
lerstand they're whoppers! If this keeps up, commuters could

have one hellish drive ahead of them in the morning. Back to Brent and Brenda.

Blowdried: Chilling stuff, Bunny. It sounds like the best bet is folks to just stay home and stay tuned right here to the Storm Advi Center.

Snowsuit: That's right, Brent. Unless you absolutely must ven out, we're urging everyone to stay off the roads—and stay glued to station for the latest developments.

Bigteeth: Good advice, Bunny. And now to give a historical perspe on just how tragic severe winter storms can be for those who ven out, national correspondent Alexa Alarmista has prepared this report.

Alarmista: Brenda, I'm standing here at the Donner Pass, where in 1 dozens of westbound commuters met slow, agonizing deaths in a sn choked mountain pass not unlike our own Schuylkill Expressway.

Bigteeth: And do I understand some actually resorted to cannibalis

Alarmista: Sadly, that's true, Brenda. Another good reason to stay h and stay glued to our live coverage. I'm Alexa Alarmista, reporting from the Donner Pass.

Blowdried: Well, we certainly don't want a repeat of that her Greater Philadelphia. Thank you, Alexa, and stay safe out there.

Bigteeth: Alexa will be back at 11 with her next installm "Avalanches—What You Need to Know."

Blowdried: Our team coverage continues with consumer repo Dennis Dumbdown, who is standing by live at the Sparkle Car Was Bucks County with a helpful snow-safety tip.

Dumbdown: With me here is Langhorne resident Shirley Yoojest has survived years of winter storms by using her wits. Shirley is goin demonstrate for us a snow-survival technique that could save your life

Yoojest (tapping foot against side of car): Well, basically, I always m a point to knock the snow off my boots before I get in my car. So people wait until they're already in their car.

Dumbdown: And by then it could be too late! That harmless b

w could be transformed in a heartbeat into a potential killer: brake-
al black ice!

Blowdried: Fascinating stuff. We now turn to meteorologist Alfie
udpuddle" Dorkman with the latest HypeU-Weather Forecast.

Dorkman: Clouds, clouds everywhere, people. Don't be lulled into
nplacency by the dry pavement. By morning, all bets could be off.

Bigteeth: Mudpuddle, am I hearing you say that tomorrow would be
excellent day to call in sick and spend the day right here with us at the
be-U-Weather Storm Advisory Center?

Dorkman: Bingo, Brenda. And now if you'll excuse me, I need to go
nt ratings—er, I mean snowflakes.

March 29, 2004

Ordinary People Vowing to Marry

many ways, they are a typical suburban couple.

They spend their weekends remodeling their tidy three-bedroom
se, which sits on a quiet street in the Main Line community of Straf-
d. They enjoy gardening and cooking and spoiling their dog, Cybil.

They both come from large, traditional Catholic families, and they dote
their 17 nieces and nephews.

Now in their early 50s, they prefer quiet nights at home to going
on the town. They pay their taxes on time, look in on sick neigh-
s, and vote each election.

They are ordinary in all ways but one: Tim Dineen and Victor Mar-
ano, a couple for nine years, are homosexuals. And that puts them
arely in the middle of the national debate on same-sex marriage.

They are not the ones protesting on courthouse steps or trying to force
nge by seeking marriage licenses where they know none will be is-
d. As the debate rages, they have written letters to newspapers, but
erwise go quietly about their suburban lives. It was for this reason—

their very ordinariness—that I sought them out last week. I wanted to
for myself just how different from the heterosexual majority a gay co
in a long-term relationship is.

Marriage of the Minds

They give me a tour of their house and show off improvements they
made—new tile, enlarged kitchen, hardwood floors. On the table is a
of pussy willows brought in from the garden. Outside, a pile of rain
ters sits in the yard, next weekend's project.

In their own minds, Dineen, a demonstration chef at a Trader
market in nearby Wayne, and Martorano, who works in the travel in
try, already are married. On their first Christmas together, they priva
exchanged gold bands that have remained on their left ring fingers
since. Still, says Dineen, "We will get married the day we legally can do

Some of the motivation is practical. If one is incapacitated, the o
right now would need a written power of attorney to make medical
cisions—a precaution they already have taken. And as Dineen pointed
over a cup of coffee, "If Victor died tomorrow, I would have to pay inI
itance tax on his half of our house."

Adds Martorano: "The law does not recognize me as his next of
and that is wrong. It's just wrong."

But more important to the couple is what marriage stands for—a p
lic acknowledgement of a couple's love and lifelong commitment. "N
riage is a stabilizing force in society," Dineen says, "and we want to be
of that stabilization."

After all, they consider themselves solid members of the commu
And so do their neighbors. As Peg Schwartz, 73 and a registered Repu
can, told me later: "I can't say enough about them. They really could
be better neighbors. They are delightful. They're just nice, kind, ca
people, and that's what you want in a neighbor." Having them next d
has softened her position on gay marriage, she said. "If that makes th
happy, then that's all that counts."

Battling Stereotypes

yet, for now at least, Dineen and Martorano will remain the one
ple on their street for whom the civil contract of marriage is not an
on. Until that day comes, the two men believe stereotypes and preju-
will continue.

Gay people have a reputation for being extremely promiscuous," says
een, whose full beard and wire-framed glasses give him a professorial
"Well, not all gay people are."

ome of them lead their lives not much differently from the straight
ple on their streets, sharing the same worries and joys and dreams. And
brings Dineen to his main point.

If we were married tomorrow, the only thing that would be
erent would be the piece of paper that grants us our rights and
onsibilities. Nothing else would change. We would still be here
as we are today, putting new gutters on the house, going to
k, grocery shopping, taking the dog to the vet."

Ie adds: "I think that's what so many people fail to realize. We're
e already. We're a couple already. For all intents and purposes, we are
ried. We just lack the legalities."

April 20, 2004

Sounds of Spring Roar in the Burbs

tside my window, it looked like the Indianapolis 500—a sure sign that
ng once again had returned to the suburbs.

rom all directions came the roar of engines, the smell of exhaust, and
violent gnashing of blades.

Yes, folks, after a long peaceful winter, that darling of the suburban
erience is back in force once again: grass-cutting season.

And last weekend, with its July-worthy temperatures, marked the

unofficial but widely observed kickoff—the ceremonial first cut. (
where I live, this is no small deal.

I knew the big day had finally arrived when I awoke Saturday to
growl of Toros and John Deeres. Homeowners, start your engines!

Outside, up and down my street, I saw the same thing: grown r
(and a few women) perched on brightly colored riding mowers, zip
gleefully across the landscape at full throttle. Grass clippings flew, and
air held that sweet perfume of gasoline mixed with crushed chlorophy

Honestly, my neighbors looked ridiculous out there, perched on t
low-riding mowing machines, knees up to their chests like so m
Shriners on go-carts.

My reaction was swift and predictable: "Dang! I've got to get
there!"

Conformity Calls

Here it was mid-April, and my tractor was still in the corner of
garage pinned beneath a pile of coiled hoses and folded lawn cha
Late again. If I didn't want to get banned from the next neighborho
potluck, I knew I had better bring my shaggy lawn into complia
pronto.

So I spent my weekend—a gorgeous weekend, perfect for hik
or bicycling or simply snoozing in a hammock—on my knees in
garage, sharpening blades, tightening belts, and changing oil. A
then with a roar and a cloud of blue smoke, I, too, was off to
races.

My lawnless friends from the city just don't get it, this communal g
fanaticism. I'm hard-pressed to explain it myself, even as I spend t
hours a week every week, April through October, embracing it.

It's totally crazy. And totally costly.

There is the price of the machines themselves, which can exc
that of a nice used automobile. There are the repairs and main
nance, the gasoline and fertilizer and pesticides. There are

:s—thousands of them each season in my subdivision alone—that
d be spent doing better things. There are the costs to the envi-
nent, both from emissions and those millions of tiny gas spills.
nd for what? A bumper crop that we neither eat nor sell nor even
 to our pets. With the fervor in which we grow this stuff, you
ld think we were all goat herders.

'e fertilize it so it will grow like crazy, then we cut like crazy just to
 up. That leaves piles of clippings, which we rake and bag beneath the
sun. And what do we do with this harvest? We place it on the curb
pay someone to haul it away.

Who's Using Whom?

makes you wonder who is actually calling the shots. Are we humans
oiting Kentucky bluegrass and fescue to tame our environment and
rove our lives? Or are the grasses exploiting us to spread their domin-
across the countryside? Think about it. When was the last time a blade
rass spent its hard-earned paycheck keeping you groomed?

 few hardy souls are fighting back. One couple I know replaced
 sod with a native wildflower meadow that required no cutting,
ertilizers, no pesticides. You want to know how well the new look
 embraced in their community? They were reported for creating a
lic nuisance.

 fight back in my own modest way, which is to say I follow the lazy
's guide to lawn care. It's strictly tough love: no fertilizers, no
nicals, no raking, no bagging. I cut it once a week, not a day more
uently.

 redictably, my lawn is a veritable United Nations of weeds. But
 all get along reasonably well, and from a passing car at a certain
d, the overall effect keeps me just this side of banishment from the
shborhood association. The difference between the über suburban
 1 and my own ragtag wannabe, I have found, comes down to this:
niles per hour.

Earth Versus the Mall People

A government spy satellite roaming the Milky Way in search of extra
restrial life has picked up a transmission coming from an unknown pla

Buzzzzzzzz. Schplunkt!

"Commander, I have just returned from my reconnaissance trip to
planet Earth."

"Ah, very good, Cygot. And what did you find there?"

"It is a strange and incomprehensible place. I landed in a confe
acy of united but deeply divided states, some red, some blue. There
a place called Joisey, where the people speak a monosyllabic gutt
dialect. And a place named Philly where the local language is e
harder to decipher. But the oddest findings came in the countrysid
a vast sprawling kingdom called Suburbia."

"What did you see in this Suburbia?"

"I saw heavily armed men dress in orange and headed out into
woods where they blasted away at anything that moved, someti
hitting each other, sometimes hitting four-legged life forms. And
at the end of each day they returned to eat an odd energy roll kno
as 'cheesesteak.'"

"Strange indeed."

"And that's just the beginning, commander. I arrived on a day ca
Thanksgiving, a tribal holiday to count blessings."

"And how do they mark this sacred day?"

"By eating vast quantities of food, sir. Some even unbutton their par

"And then what do they do with all this energy they have consume

"They sleep, sir."

A Predawn Sojourn

"A sort of hibernation?"

"Not exactly. The feast appears to be the start of a vast national rathon they call 'Just 29 Shopping Days to Christmas.' Within rs they are up again, and they head off in darkness to giant edi-s surrounded by acres of a gray stonelike surface."

"Their sacred temples, no doubt."

"Yes, and they call these temples all the same name: Mall. The rshippers wait for hours to get inside the doors."

"And what do they do once inside?"

"They use small plastic cards to spend riches they do not have for ds they do not need."

"Goods they do not need?"

"Such as clear stones the slave class digs from the earth."

"They pay vast sums for mere stones?"

"The males hand them to the females who then agree to bear their geny."

"A fertility rite! And what else?"

"The females wear ceremonial gold and buy expensive pouches to d their plastic cards. They buy paint for their faces and many pairs of her coverings for their feet."

"Why many pairs when they have but one pair of feet?"

"Inexplicable, commander, but their closets overflow with them. And men fill their garages with the lumbering personal transporters wn as SUVs, which suck finite fossil fuels from the ground and force nations to battle each other."

Zombie Nation

d who commands them to buy these useless things?"

"The orders come from the Great Persuaders, who rule from a place d Madison Avenue. They decide what the masses must buy and send sages through the electronic tubes in every dwelling, telling the ple they are nothing without these items."

And the people fall for this?"

"No questions asked, sir. Especially during the Christmas 29-
marathon."

"And how is this race won?"

"It seems the household with the most items on Christmas Day is
winner."

"And how do they celebrate?"

"I am told they will awaken before dawn the day after and return
the mall temples, where they exchange the many things they acqu
during the marathon for yet more possessions."

"And they do this to celebrate this day they call Christmas?"

"They call it a religious holiday."

"And what is this day? Surely, it must stand for more than that wh
the plastic card can obtain."

"It once did, I am told, commander. But the people became blin
at the mall temples, and the original meaning appears to have been
long ago."

"Cygot, your excellent surveillance disturbs me greatly. Now to the
contamination unit before the Earthling consumption disease gets loo

December 13, 2

Tow-Truck Driver Became Her Angel

What had begun as just another family reunion at Philadelphia Inter
tional Airport escalated quickly into a life-or-death race against the cl

Mary Helene Wagner, 78, had just arrived at the airport at c
November 9 after an uneventful flight from her home in Oakland, C
fornia. Waiting to greet her at the gate were her sister, Katherine "K
Colucci, 65, and Kitti's husband, Richard, of Little Egg Harbor, near
lantic City.

The threesome chatted as they loaded Wagner's bags into the Colu
car in the parking garage.

That's when it happened.

"Kitti suddenly cried out in pain and put her hands to her forehead," gner said. She moaned about an excruciating headache and began to nit.

"She started to scream, 'My head, my head,'" Colucci's husband added. "I knew we had to move," the older sister said. "I said to Richard, 'We e to get to an emergency room.'"

3ut where, and how? None of them were familiar with Philadelphia, . there was no one in sight to ask. They drove out of the garage and :d the parking attendant for directions, but because of a language bar-, they could not understand what he was trying to tell them.

They headed off into the darkness, knowing each lost minute could ke a terrible difference. "I was looking around; I didn't know the area ll. I realized we were in trouble," Richard Colucci said.

A Brief Touch

pulled into an Exxon station and frantically asked a customer for di- ions, but again without luck. His wife was again vomiting out of the cradling her head.

That's when Wagner spotted the least likely of guardian angels—a mber of that profession area motorists love to hate: a Greater Philly -truck driver. He was filling the gas tank on his big lime-green cker, and Wagner figured he must know the way to the nearest pital.

"I approached him for help. He was trying to tell me what to do, but I ik he could see the look on my face," she said. "He reached out and ched me, put his hand on my shoulder and said, 'Follow me.'"

Yellow emergency lights flashing, the driver led them through rush-hour fic, winding his way across the city until he pulled up at the emergency- m doors of the Hospital of the University of Pennsylvania. The driver itated just long enough to make sure the Coluccis reached the curb.

"He tooted his horn, turned off his [emergency] lights, and just drove away," Wagner said. "We never saw the side of the truck, the name anything."

All she knew of the mystery man was his first name, James.

Only after they were inside did they fully realize just what a cru role the stranger had played in the emergency. Not only had he quic led Kitti Colucci, who had suffered a triple ruptured brain aneurysm, t hospital, he led her to the right hospital.

As one of the nation's top medical centers, HUP had a team of neur ogists on duty to begin immediate aid when the Coluccis walked in.

An Angel in Disguise?

Doctors confirmed that in such a case, every second counted. Without tow-truck driver's intervention, Richard Colucci said, "most likely K would have died. We'll never know for sure."

More than a month later, she remains hospitalized and faces long re bilitation. But she is alive, and her husband and sister won't forget kind stranger.

"I want him to know we are very grateful," Wagner said. "I hate think about what would have happened had we [stopped at the gas tion] and James hadn't been there."

Richard Colucci believes it was more than coincidence. "I person feel that somebody upstairs was looking out for us," he said. "This fell was there for a purpose."

He wished he could find the driver.

"I would embrace him if I could. I would thank him, and I would him that he was an angel," Colucci said.

"That might sound corny, but I really mean it. You have to understa we were looking at life and death."

Colucci might get his chance.

Tomorrow, I will introduce you to the mystery Good Samaritan, tell you how I located him.

December 14, 2004

James Pratt
A Knight in a Lime-Green Tow Truck

e Good Samaritan in the lime-green tow truck is a mystery no more.

His name is James Pratt, and he is a 30-year-old single dad who duated from Germantown High School, Class of '91, and served in ▪ army in Germany before earning a discharge because of a bad ▪k. He now lives in Conshohocken with his daughter. "She turns 5 Christmas Day," he said.

Pratt makes his living patrolling a stretch of I-95 under contract with ▪ Pennsylvania Department of Transportation, swooping in to help ▪nded motorists and remove disabled vehicles to keep traffic moving.

He was just ending his shift on the evening of November 9 when ▪ pulled into the Airport Exxon station at Philadelphia International ▪port to refuel.

That's when his life intersected with the lives of Mary Helene Wagner, ▪ of Oakland, California; Wagner's sister, Kitti Colucci, 65, of Little Egg ▪rbor, New Jersey; and Kitti's husband, Richard.

As I described yesterday, the Coluccis had just picked up Wagner from ▪iladelphia International Airport when Kitti Colucci was struck without ▪rning by a searing, violent headache and vomiting, the result, she ▪uld later learn, of a triple ruptured brain aneurysm. The three were lost ▪ in desperate need of a hospital.

Wagner ran up to the tow-truck driver, and he began to give her ▪ections. But two things became immediately clear to Pratt: Every ▪ond was of the essence, and the frantic travelers were not going to ▪ able to find the hospital on their own.

"Follow me," he told her and then, yellow lights flashing, led the

family through rush-hour traffic to the Hospital of the University
Pennsylvania where more than one month later Kitti Colucci conti
ues to recover.

The Coluccis and Wagner were grateful to the tow-truck driver w
led them to the front doors of the hospital, but they had no way of telli
him so. He had vanished without giving them anything but his first nar
And so Wagner called me.

Based on the little she knew—a lime-green truck and an Exxon s
tion near the terminal—I was able to find Pratt through his boss, Ke
Bowe, a Conshohocken-based tow operator who runs Airport Exxon a
has the PennDot Expressway Safety Service Patrol contract.

"I'm not really surprised," Bowe said when told of his employee's
tions to help the stricken woman. "He's a good guy."

Pratt downplayed what he had done. He was about to drive back
Conshohocken anyway, he said, and the hospital was not that big a
tour.

"I just told them to follow my lights," he recalled. "I got them to t
front door of the hospital and kept going. I never heard anything after t
fact."

When I told him that Richard Colucci had credited his good de
with saving his wife's life, Pratt hesitated a moment before saying, "Th
a pleasant plus. It's a beautiful thing to know." He had no idea just h
significant his small act of kindness was to these desperate strangers w
had stumbled upon him.

As a tow-truck driver, he said, he is either loved or hated. Loved
those who are stranded and he rescues; hated by those who are parked
legally and he tows. "You learn to take the good with the bad," he said

Helping the Coluccis in their moment of need, he added, was one
the good moments that "helps your job balance itself out."

And it served as a reminder to us all that even in a city as proudly gr
as Philadelphia, in an age when people too often shrug off getting i

ed, at a time when too many ask, "What's in it for me?" there are still
e knights among us who don't hesitate to come to the rescue of per-
strangers simply because it is the right and decent thing to do.

It shows that there still are good people in this world," a grateful
ard Colucci said.

esponded Pratt as he headed to his next call: "Hey, it's no prob-
. That's what I do. That's why I'm out here."

February 1, 2005

Zero Tolerance Running Amok

ay's question: How can we adults expect our children to respect us
our decisions when so often we act like total blockheads?

ow can we ask them to accept our edicts without question when too
n those edicts, however well-intentioned, are so wildly misguided?

ake zero-tolerance policies in our schools. They are in place for a
on. Weapons and drugs have no place in schools. But the words
and tolerance, when combined, add up to one scary concept: blind
rcement with no room for common sense.

nd when that happens, what are we left with? Injustice. And kids
lose faith and grow jaded. No wonder they look at us like we were
beamed down from Planet Clueless.

xhibit A: The case of the crampy honors student.

s reported by Stephanie L. Arnold in Saturday's *Inquirer*, a senior on
honor roll at Haverford High School had the temerity to take an
r-the-counter pain medication—a generic version of Aleve—for
strual cramps without first clearing it with the school nurse.

ind you, she is 18, old enough to fight and die in Iraq. Mind
, she was not misusing the pain medicine. Mind you, she made no
mpt to hide her behavior. In fact, she was busted after she went to

the nurse and reported that her cramping continued, despite the
she took.

A World Without Grays

Does this sound like a crazed drug abuser to you? In the black-and-w
world of zero tolerance, the question is moot. She violated the sch
drug policy, which bans students from, among other things, taking m
cation without permission. And she was suspended, if only for part of
day, before she apologized and was allowed back in school.

The girl's mother about nailed it when she likened the policy
"throwing a hand grenade on an anthill."

Unfortunately, the problem is not isolated, which leads to Exhibit
The case of the handcuffed 10-year-old.

Porsche Brown, a fourth grader at Holme Elementary Schoo
Northeast Philadelphia, was suspended after an 8-inch pair of scissors
found in her book bag. But the saga did not end there. Police arri
handcuffed the pint-size fugitive, and carted her down to the l
precinct house in the back of a police wagon.

Geez, I'd hate to see what they would have done had she been pack
a stapler and Elmer's glue.

It's more than a little ridiculous. It's plain dumb. Everyone agrees
child meant no harm in bringing the scissors to school. Yet, at the ti
the police policy was to cuff all weapons suspects, regardless of age. An
a child was treated like a criminal.

Schools chief Paul Vallas and city Police Commissioner Sylve
Johnson later apologized to the girl's mother, admitting the princ
and cops overreacted. Ya think?

A Syrup-Crusted Blade

And, finally, consider Exhibit C: The case of the sticky eating utensil.

This one involves yet another honors student, Peter DeWitt, a senic
Great Valley High School in Chester County. DeWitt's car was singled

a drug search in the school's parking lot in September. No drugs were
nd, but authorities did spot a small penknife and a steak knife.

DeWitt explained that he used the penknife to tinker with his car
eo. The steak knife had been used by his sister, who ate a plate of waf-
in the car on the way to school with him. The parents—who, by sup-
ng the waffles, I suppose were accessories to the crime—confirmed
story.

he alleged weapons never even left the confines of the locked
 Harmless enough, you say? Sorry, no room for reason. Under
 tolerance, DeWitt faced possible expulsion until cooler heads
vailed three days into his suspension.

n each of these cases lurks a glimmer of justification. Children can and
harm themselves by improperly taking medications. Children can and
use something as innocuous as scissors or a utensil to harm others.

here should be no room in schools for harmful behavior of any type.
 there should be room for common sense, discretion, and intelligence.
f we want our kids to respect authority, we owe them that much.

March 14, 2005

It's Unhealthy, But It Is Legal

en I was 10, my best friend and I rode our bikes to the local bowling
, slipped 35 cents into the vending machine, and bought our first pack
igarettes.

n the woods nearby, we lit up—and promptly turned green. I decided
 and there that if this was what it took to be cool, I'd gladly go
ugh life as a dweeb.

o this day, I have little tolerance for cigarette smoke and even less for
e inconsiderate slobs who think it is their God-given right to light up
ime, anyplace—and then toss their butts wherever they might fall.

confess I'm annoyed by smokers in the workplace who spend 10

minutes of every hour out in the parking lot puffing away on breaks th
nonsmoking colleagues do not enjoy.

Basically I hate everything about cigarettes. So why am I so unco
fortable with the growing national jihad against smokers?

It might have something to do with the fact that cigarette smokin
legal. Unhealthy, dangerous, stupid, but legal nonetheless.

And yet we increasingly treat cigarettes as contraband and those v
indulge in them as social pariahs.

Cities are lining up to ban smoking in public gathering places, incl
ing bars and taverns, where smoking and drinking often go hand in ha
The Philadelphia City Council is set to vote Thursday on a widespr
smoking prohibition. Mayor Street said he'd like to see a nationwide b

Workplace Litmus Test

And perhaps most troubling of all, Montgomery County is explorin
policy that would bar the hiring of smokers for county jobs.

We allegedly live in a free country, and that means having the freed
to indulge in harmful behavior. People smoke and drink too much a
eat greasy burgers instead of salads and lounge in front of the televis
instead of exercising. And they will die younger because of it. Th
choice.

Do we really want to go down this road of regulating legal but u
healthy behavior? If you want to take away my french fries, you'll have
pry them out of my cold, dead hand.

No one should be forced to breathe secondhand smoke, and smok
bans in workplaces, stores, and government buildings make perfect sen

But if a bunch of smokers want to sit in a smoke-filled bar and suck
one another's carbon monoxide over beer, shouldn't they have that rig
I won't be there, but I respect their right to turn their lungs into tar p:

Conversely, nonsmokers are free to choose smoke-free establishme
to eat and drink. And the more they vote with their pocketbooks,
more clean-air joints will open.

Let the marketplace decide.

Freedom to Choose

pub near my home went smoke-free last year, not because government
t a gun to its head but because the owner saw money to be made.
lost the chain-smoking drinkers and gained the bigger-spending
ne-and-dinner crowd.

When the place reeked of smoke, I chose to stay away; now I'm a
ular. Isn't that how it should work?

Montgomery County thinks it can save on health-care costs if it refuses
hire smokers. But wouldn't it make more sense to simply charge smok-
; employees a higher premium for health insurance? If they want to
oke, fine, but let them pay their way. If you have ever tried to buy life
surance, you know the stiff premiums smokers face. Fair enough.

What Montgomery County, or any employer, should really be
ncerned about is finding the best possible employee. Do you turn
wn a hard worker with a sterling resume and references because he
okes? Do you hire a nonsmoking slacker instead?

If cigarettes are really that harmful—and we all know they are—let's
tlaw them. That might, after all, actually send an unmuddied message to
r children about what we really think of these cancer sticks.

That, of course, will never happen, not so long as the tobacco industry
Congress eating out of its hand.

Before we start placing smokers in the public stocks, we might want to
e a second look at that $10 billion (yes, billion) buyout Congress ap-
oved for tobacco growers last fall.

Isn't it all just a little hypocritical?

March 18, 20

The Nonsense Logic of Angry Smokers

The smokers are restless.

Agitated, defensive, defiant, at times shrill, definitely ticked off. Th
habit is under assault from all directions.

The Philadelphia City Council yesterday tabled a vote to joi
growing list of cities around the country that have banned smoki
in public places, including that onetime smoker's haven, the corr
tappy. Montgomery County wants to save on health insurance costs
refusing to hire smokers. And in New Jersey, lawmakers are advanci
their own smoking crackdown.

Like any cornered animal, smokers are lashing out. I know. I've be
getting an earful.

Take, for example, the message left on my voice mail by Ang
Smoker No. 1. She wants us to know tobacco for her is not a m
vice but a professional necessity. "Tobacco relaxes the nerves," she sa
"It is something as an artist and a blues singer that I require for
job. I require a raspy voice; I require the effects of nicotine after ea
sculpture and painting."

Doesn't prefer it, mind you. Positively requires it. Just like the bott
oxygen she someday will be requiring.

Angry Smoker No. 1 argues that banning smoking in public pla
is just the start of a downward spiral into "prejudice and Nazism a
fascism."

As she predicts: "OK, anyone 150 pounds overweight can't go i
any restaurants; they're too fat and risk a heart attack. Also, all peo
who eat chocolate should be condemned because they're causing cavi
and diabetes. And we should ban sugar. No sugar in coffee or tea!"

Cry, Baby, Cry

…d while we're at it, might I suggest we ban whining crybabies?

Somehow, in her nicotine-addled brain, all bad habits are equal.
…ewing fingernails or mainlining heroin, it doesn't matter.

Then came Angry Smoker No. 2: "All children should be refused food
…they are obese. All children who are obese should not be fed in the
…chroom. They are a health risk and insurance will go up for them."

And angry Smoker No. 3: "I think we should outlaw everyone who
…s tuna fish, because the secondhand fumes from tuna cause ill health
…ects and make people throw up."

Cough … hack … wheeze.

Secondhand smoke, secondhand food odors—no difference at all.
…t a bit. Same health risks, same watery eyes, same stench in your hair
…d clothes at the end of the day.

Not all smokers are this delusional. Several I heard from said they try
…d to be considerate and only smoke where they won't bother others.
…hers told me they are not proud of their ways, but they reminded me it
… powerful addiction.

I know many smokers who indeed are trying to quit and are very
…nsiderate—so considerate, in fact, I sometimes forget they are smokers
…ll.

They just want to be left to puff in peace. Is that so bad? As I wrote
…nday, I hate the smoke but love the smoker. I say if smokers want to
…wd together in bars to inhale each others' soot, that should be their
…rogative.

A Little Honesty, Please

…t I also expect smokers to be honest with themselves and everyone
….

When you insist on smoking in a closed car with your three kids buckled beside you, forced to suck your fumes, don't ask for sympathy.

When you light up in a "smoking section" that is feet from the "no smoking section" with nothing but an imaginary line separating the tv know you are ruining someone's meal.

When you toss your butts out your car windows, know you are a p

When you stand in the doorway of a smoke-free building to get yo fix, know you are making the rest of us run a foul gauntlet.

When you sneak a few quick puffs in the office rest-room, know t we know. Hours later, we still know.

When you ask, "Mind if I smoke?" even as you're striking the mat realize that most of us will say "no" out of politeness but mean "yes."

There are many considerate smokers out there. They are not the pr lem. It's the inconsiderate ones, willfully blind to the effect their habit on others, who have forced the issue and brought this whole natio backlash upon themselves.

Puff on that, angry smokers.

May 9, 20

A Shared Concern for a Jane Doe

Jane Doe is nameless no more.

She died, homeless and unmissed, one year ago this week after a accidentally backed into her in a parking lot in downtown Allentown.

Her lice-infested clothes were burned, her body laid unceremoniou in a pauper's field just off Interstate 78 in the shadow of a concrete pla A small laminated card on a metal stake was her only headstone: "J Doe, May 12, 2004, County of Lehigh."

And she likely would have forever remained unidentified if not for t

men who had never met but who both showed kindness to a lost soul
unted by mental illness.

Suzanne Kratzer, a retired eighth-grade teacher in Allentown, and
yllis Graham, a retired nurse in Plymouth Meeting, stumbled into each
er's lives after Jane Doe's death and pieced together the clues that
uld solve the mystery.

The clues stretched back a half century to when Graham was in
rsing school at the former Germantown Hospital in Philadelphia.
r roommate and close friend for three years was a petite brunette
m the town of Mount Carmel in the Poconos.

Her name: Leona Kovalick.

"She was just really a cute kid," Graham remembered, "bubbly,
ervescent, fun-loving, carefree."

Carefree Days

e two double-dated and spent summer Saturdays on the beach in
ean City. "We had tons of fun, but she never would talk about her
kground," Graham said.

Graham was married in 1950, and her old roommate attended. "That
s the last time I ever saw her," she said.

But Graham occasionally received letters from Kovalick, and as the
rs passed she could tell her old friend was becoming something
ond eccentric. Kovalick was always vague about where she lived
d rebuffed Graham's efforts to visit her.

Enter Kratzer, the retired teacher who, while walking her dog near her
me one evening in 2002, spotted a tiny, weathered woman lying on the
ch of an office building, a large bag of clothing beside her. "I walked
and asked her if she was all right," Kratzer recalled. "It was nearly dark,
I was concerned for her safety. I asked if she'd had any dinner."

Kratzer would later return with a plate of food. She began aiding the
meless woman she knew as Lee, helping her secure widow's benefits

through the Department of Veterans Affairs and trying unsuccessfully

persuade her to check into a shelter.

She also let the woman use her mailing address to receive letters.

After the woman disappeared off the streets in April 2004, Krat:

opened a card that had arrived for Leona Kovalick. It was from Graham

A String of Clues

The two women compared notes. They had both read about the unide

tified Jane Doe: Kratzer in her local paper; Graham in this column. T

more they talked, the more certain they were of Jane Doe's identity.

Graham remembered that Kovalick had told her she had a nephew

Louisiana. Graham located him, and he contacted the Lehigh Cou

Coroner's office, which sent him a photograph of the unidentifi

woman.

"I immediately knew it was her," J. Richard Kanuch, a lawyer in N

Orleans, said. An old X-ray from an arm fracture Kanuch remembered

aunt suffering provided a positive match, said Paul Zondlo, Lehi

County's chief deputy coroner.

Kanuch said his aunt had grown erratic and irascible by the time s

was in her 30s. She could be sweet one moment and hostile the next. F

hygiene had become poor, and she could be physically abusive, he sa

One by one, she alienated all 12 of her siblings. Eventually, she just va

ished.

"I don't know what happened to her," he said. "She went through c

lege; she did very well in nursing, dated several surgeons. . . . It's a

story."

At noon Thursday, on the first anniversary of her death, the won

once known as Jane Doe will get a proper send-off. Kratzer, Graham, a

a handful of Graham's nursing-school classmates will gather graveside.

A priest will say a few words. There will be flowers and a real he

stone inscribed with a real name:

Leona Kovalick Bosker, June 1, 1928, to May 12, 2004.

May 13, 2005

A Friend Lost in Life, but Found in Death

llis Graham stood by the small headstone in a pauper's field a few
es outside Allentown yesterday and opened the leather-bound
book from Germantown Hospital's Class of 1948.

ive of her nursing-school classmates from that year, all long retired,
ered around to see.

There she is," Graham said, pointing to a black-and-white photograph
n attractive, petite woman in a white uniform, her chin upturned
tly. "That's Lee."

eona Kovalick Bosker. She was born June 1, 1928, and grew up in
nsylvania coal country. She died one year ago yesterday, an
dentified, lice-infested homeless woman crushed by a van as she
dled in a parking space.

Vhat a long, sad journey it was.

s the yearbook playfully described her: "Here she is, the 'Blonde
nber' of our class. She loves clothes and can really do them justice. Lee
e life of every party and possesses a certain personal charm that can't
eaten and a laugh that can't be mistaken."

he yearbook entry for Bosker concludes: "We know we need
wish her luck because it's already headed her way." But nothing
mbling luck graced the life of this woman whose once bright future
nmeted into the depths of self-destructive mental illness.

he women arrived at the indigent cemetery just before noon with a
ed geranium and a bouquet of lilies-of-the-valley to place by their
er classmate's grave. They wanted to give her a proper send-off. They
ted to remember her as what she once had been, not as what she had
me.

"I couldn't bear to see her go that way," Graham said. "None o
wanted to see her buried like that."

Buried alone and unmissed in a pressboard box, a nameless, face
vagrant designated by Lehigh County authorities simply as Jane D
The woman with no name.

It took the better part of a year, but Graham and a retired Allento
schoolteacher, Suzanne Kratzer, who had befriended the home
woman on the streets of Allentown in 2002, pieced together the clues
allowed authorities to positively identify the former nurse.

Now her old classmates, who had not seen Bosker in more than h
century, gathered to say goodbye.

"She was a fun-loving kid, happy-go-lucky," recalled Audrey Rab
Bethlehem.

"Very outgoing, fun to be with," added Betty Salevsky of New Ho

Graham recalled giggling with Lee late into the night in their dor
tory—and losing their privileges because of it. She talked of sneaking
for ice cream, window shopping along Germantown Avenue, double-
ing, and returning sunburned from beach trips.

Madeleine Bowen of Willow Grove said Leona could make her c
mates laugh. She remembered one incident in particular. Tea enemas v
sometimes used in those days to help sick children, and the first t
Leona was ordered to administer one, she looked up and asked: "Do I
sugar and lemon in it?"

"All the girls howled about that," Bowen said. "She was serious. Th
what was so funny about it."

All the women agreed they never saw any signs to make them sus
their former classmate's life could possibly one day come so unrave
And yet it did. An utterly ordinary life come utterly undone.

Soon, a priest arrived. The group had invited him, because Bo
had been raised Catholic. The Rev. Harold Dagle, pastor of Immacu
Conception Church in Allentown, stood beneath the wind-whip
sky and told the small group that this woman was one of the many

ls we pass on the streets every day. "And yet, somehow in death," he
ed, "she was found."

he priest prayed, "Eternal rest grant unto her, O Lord, and perpetual
t shine upon her."

he women, standing in a circle clutching their flowers and pho-
aphs and memories, responded: "Amen."

hen Graham, her voice choking, said, "We had three years together—
hed a lot, cried a lot, but cared a lot about each other, too. Goodbye,
"

June 7, 2005

Honked Off by Bumper Sticker

as one of those days on the Pennsylvania Turnpike. Hot, muggy,
ded—and then came the dreaded red sea of brake lights.

My morning commute had barely begun yesterday when a Turnpike
mission truck with a flashing sign announced the bad news: "Prepare
op. Accident ahead." Far ahead.

raffic screeched to a standstill; twin ribbons of stopped cars
ched to the horizon, as if I had stumbled into the world's largest
llel-parking competition. There we sat, my fellow commuters and
king in the sun, our dress shirts wilting, out blood pressure rising.
ether, we formed a sea of hot and bothered humanity, all late.

t was into this cauldron that Mr. Cheerful merged in his white SUV.
nudged his way in front of me, and that's when I saw it—a bumper
er affixed prominently to the vehicle's rear window, right at eye level.
And what was his cheery message to his fellow road warriors?

Was it "Have a nice day"?

Was it "If you're happy and you know it, beep your horn"?

Was it "We're all in this together"?

Not even close. His bumper sticker read: "I want to kill you."

Great. I'm trapped on a slab of smoldering pavement, my gas nee
edging toward E, the sweat trickling between my shoulder blades—
this Einstein wants to kill me. Just the pick-me-up I was looking for
this swell Monday morning.

Mutual Contempt

"Want to kill me?" I muttered. "Not as bad as I want to kill you, pal."

Actually, I used a word considerably more colorful than pal. What ca
say? Incivility breeds incivility.

Through the back window, I could see him jawboning on his
phone, free hand drumming the steering wheel. This was not a h
school kid trying to get attention; not a college-age student wit
warped sense of humor. The guy was old enough to know better.

I want to kill you. What kind of public statement was that?

Did he think he was being funny? Provocative? Outrageous?

Given the message's position at eye level and its small type, I guesse
was aimed at tailgaters. Some of those slogans can be a hoot, like the
that goes: "If you can read this, you are within firing range."

That's witty. "I want to kill you" is only creepy and sociopathic. A
with the number of road-rage assaults and homicides ticking ever upw
it's just a little chilling.

I wonder whether Douglas Heavlow, now in prison, sported one
those signs in his pickup truck the day in 2000 he intention
sideswiped a car he thought was going too slow on the turnpi
Northeast Extension, killing a 21-year-old woman.

Or the enraged trucker on Route 22 in Northampton County, sen
prison for intentionally ramming his rig into the back of another vehi
killing two men.

Part of the Problem

the guy who fatally stabbed another man with a sword during a
-rage confrontation in Camden. Or the countless hotheads who
pointed, even fired, guns at other drivers.

want to kill you.

oo often, the threat is real.

had more than a half hour to sit, contemplating Mr. Cheerful's
icidal proclamation, and here is what I finally decided I would like
ell him:

isten, buddy, no one is laughing. When you treat me with respect and
ity, I'll treat you the same. When you're considerate, I'll be consider-
When you open your arms to me as a fellow sufferer in the commuter
, I'll embrace you back.

ut when you tell me, and everyone around me, how little you value
lives, please know that you are something worse than just a coarse and
le (and not very original) cretin. You, Mr. Cheerful, are part of the
lem. You are the abrasive that has turned society so rough and ugly.

the battle between incivility and decency, between goonishness and
leness, between those who build community and those who tear it
t, you are the enemy.

o do Greater Philadelphia a favor. Take your little bumper sticker,
. . . and . . . have a nice day, sir. Now, how hard was that?

July 25, 2005

When Our Fears Lead to Prejudices

sin of prejudice paid me a little visit last week.

Jo, I'm not proud of myself.

was visiting New York City and arrived at the Port Authority late in
afternoon to grab an express bus back to Pennsylvania. On my way

into the terminal, I passed a knot of National Guardsmen in camoufl
automatic rifles slung over their shoulders. They chatted among th
selves as the masses streamed by, many like myself toting packages
suitcases. It occurred to me that there was little they could do to
someone whose bag just might hold a bomb.

The bus was nearly full. Just as it was about to pull out, a last-mi
passenger clambered aboard carrying a large rectangular package wrap
in a black trash bag. He kept his eyes down and sat in the only remai
seat, directly in front of me.

I felt an immediate, visceral response to his presence. My heart be
to race, my stomach to tighten. I could feel the blood coursing thro
my temples.

The man was young, probably 19 or 20, with short black hair ar
closely trimmed beard. He appeared to be of Middle Eastern ancestry

Oh God . . . a suicide bomber.

Calculus of Terror

Instantly, I told myself I was being ridiculous—and horrible. I kr
nothing about this stranger, who may have been a college studen
engineer or son on his way home to visit his parents. All I knew
that he somehow, at least at this moment, reminded me ominousl
the faces of the young Muslim men who had detonated bomb
London on July 7, killing themselves and 52 others.

The more I tried to dismiss the notion, the more unnerved I beca
It all made perfect sense to me. He was traveling alone (yes, and so wa
he was gripping a large package with both hands. At least to my eyes
appeared nervous, uncomfortable. It occurred to me only later that
discomfort might have had something to do with the fact that people
me were presuming him to be evil based solely on his heritage.

Still, the pieces fit. Young, Islamic (I presumed) man. Alone, grippin
odd, bulky package. On a crowded bus that in about three minutes wo
be deep inside the Lincoln Tunnel. At rush hour.

First London. Now, once again, New York. A one-two punch. Of

urse!

As the bus approached the tunnel entrance, an acid burn rose from my

. Fear, the likes of which I had not experienced in years.

An Unfair Assumption

as less than three feet from him. If a bomb went off, I wouldn't

e a chance, wouldn't even know it. One moment I would be

ndering. The next I would be gone.

glanced around. If any of the other passengers harbored similar

givings, they weren't showing it. But then, neither was I.

like to think of myself as open-minded. I like to think I judge

lividuals on their merits. Yet here I was, ready to sprint to the

nt of the bus and demand the driver let me off. And for what?

Was this any different from the white woman who panics when a black

n steps onto an elevator with her? No, it was not. I was guilty. Guilty of

judging. Of racial profiling. Of stereotyping.

knew that. Still, the terror was real. As we descended into the

nel, I squeezed my eyes shut. If a terrorist were aboard, this is

ere he would act. An eternity later, we emerged into sunlight. I've

ver been so happy to see New Jersey. The man was still sitting

re, gripping his package. I began to relax, but then he opened the

stic bag and began fumbling inside. Another wave of dread. Another

e alarm.

By the time I stepped off the bus at my stop, my would-be terrorist

s asleep. It was now clear: He was just a guy going somewhere—no

ferent from me. I stepped off the bus, whispering an apology only I

ald hear.

The terrorist assault on free societies has many, many victims. Not all of

m are hit by shrapnel and flying nails.

Curse the terrorists for what they have done. Shame on me for what I

e allowed them to do.

A Terrorist? Moi? Twice Exonerated

I'm not the world's most imposing man, so when I was yanked out of li
at Philadelphia International Airport Saturday for a special head-to-t
full-terrorist-alert search, I must confess to mixed emotions.

Part of me was annoyed. I had a flight to catch; what was this all abo
Did I look like a terrorist?

Part of me was impressed. The Transportation Safety Administrati
screeners were professional and courteous—a definite step up from
private security drones they replaced after 9/11, most of whom left
impression they had just been recruited from the Burger King take-
window.

Part of me was relieved. If a middle-age dad like me could merit su
scrutiny, what chance did a real terrorist have of getting through?

And part of me was—yes, I'll admit it—a little flattered. This mig
well have been the first time in my life that someone considered m
threat to anything. As the TSA screener ran his beeping scanner o
me, I couldn't help standing a little taller. Wow, they think I just mig
be dangerous!

Something on my boarding pass had set them off, a dreaded four-di
code. As soon as I showed it to the first guard, he opened the gate and polit
said, "Follow me, please." He walked me into a fenced corral and called
for a male scanner to pat me down. Gee, I didn't get a choice?

Assume the Position

As he snapped on his latex gloves, the pat-down expert calmly explain
what he was about to do. I kicked off my shoes and assumed the positi
on the two footprints glued to the floor, my arms out in a messianic po

nbuckle your belt," he ordered. Yikes! The banjo theme music from
liverance played in my head.

Officer Pat-Down ran his hands around my waist, back and sides and
and down each leg, skirting dangerously close to that off-limits zone
mother always told me was no one's business but my own.

He had me roll down the waistband of my jeans, as if I might be hid-
a Kalashnikov in there, and worked it over like he was kneading
ugh.

Meanwhile, his female colleague had my carry-on luggage splayed
en and was poking through my socks, underwear, and toiletries. All I
uld think was, Please, Lord, don't let my wife's pantyhose be in there.

It was not even 7 a.m., and I was getting felt up by one stranger while
other was fluffing my boxer shorts. All while my fellow passengers filed
t, gawking and no doubt wondering what dark secrets I must hold to
rit such scrutiny.

The female screener rubbed a cloth pad over all surfaces of my luggage
l belongings, inside and out, and then ran the pad through a sensor in
rch of trace amounts of explosives.

"Follow Me, Please," Again?

veral minutes later, I was deemed no risk to anyone whatsoever—
re's a news flash—and left to buckle up and gather my belongings.

One random search I can live with. This is part of our duty as
nericans in the post–9/11 age, to put up with these small humiliations
d curtailments on our freedom in the name of safety for all.

But the next day, as I approached the security checkpoint in Chicago
come home, I was greeted by the same polite "Will you follow me,
ase?" and subjected to the same top-to-bottom search of my body and
longings. What was going on?

I asked the screener, and he had no idea. Many things could trigger a
rch, he said. Had I paid cash for my ticket? Bought it at the last minute?

Was it only one-way? None of the above. "Or it might just be random," the screener told me.

Twice in two days?

I thought about blaming my travel agent. It was my first time using her, and I pictured her adding an addendum to my ticket purchase: "I'd keep an eye on this creep if I were you."

Perhaps it had something to do with the fact that my ticket was paid by a third party—my book publisher—and involved such a short stay.

What I do know is this: If the automatic triggers that ensnared me twice in two days also pinpoint would-be terrorists, the hassle and humiliation are all worth it. I'll assume the position without complaint.

But that's a considerable if.

December 6, 20

Even Vicki Needs to Work on Image

I was sitting in the Granite Run Mall near Media Saturday, doing what married men everywhere do while their wives are off giving the Visa card a good, plastic-melting, pre-holiday workout.

I sat and stared at the Victoria's Secret mannequin.

Actually, she stared at me; I merely returned her unblinking gaze.

Vicki, as I named her, was hard to miss. She stood right in the front window under bright lights, balancing precariously on spike heels, curly blonde hair cascading over her shoulders. She was tall enough to play in the NBA with legs as long and fluid as the Schuylkill. She was as close to naked as one can get in public without risking arrest.

Her wardrobe consisted of a hot-pink Santa hat with matching hot-pink bra and tiny, tiny, tiny panties.

"Good Lord, there's not enough there for a decent hanky," I started to say before realizing I was sounding like my grandmother again.

I suppose it's a sure sign of middle age when you begin channeling

g-departed relatives. One day you're young and worldly and rolling
r eyes at the insufferable things grown-ups say; the next you are
nelessly stealing all their best lines.

Barbie, All Grown Up

d to admit, Vicki was fetching, just like a life-size Barbie doll, only
er. Her features were even more exaggerated, the mile-long legs,
ossibly small waist, and swelling bosom. Vicki's hip bones jutted
 beneath a flat, sunken stomach; her arms were like matchsticks. If
 idealized female miraculously came to life, she'd need to be
ied to the anorexia ward of the nearest hospital.

And we wonder why so many teenage girls have eating disorders and
-esteem issues?

Still, women of all ages flocked into the store, picking over the tiny
ments. It goes without saying that there was a major disconnect be-
en the plaster beauty in the window and those drawn in by her.

The shoppers came in all shapes and sizes. They were round and
r-shaped, droopy and angular, tall and short. Most, to be honest, even
 teens, were varying degrees of overweight, a reflection of today's
rfed and under-exerted America. The few I spotted who looked
py enough to actually get away with wearing the revealing outfits in
 front window turned out to be middle-school age. Yikes!

Believe me, if there were a Victor's Secret in the mall with an idealized
le hunk in the window, we men wouldn't hold up any better.

 I swear I could single-handedly put Speedo out of business with but
 brief beach stroll in one of its stamp-size swimsuits.)

n other words, unlike the robo-model in the window, the shoppers in
 mall Saturday were human.

And we humans, fueled on supersize fast foods and bucket-size soft
nks, are getting fatter by the hour. Not just the adults but the children,
. Childhood obesity has more than doubled over the last 25 years.

Reality-Fantasy Chasm

And, for once, metropolitan Philadelphia is a leading cultural trendse·
All hail the caloric cheesesteak!

What are we doing about it? Gawking at life-size fantasy dolls ·
hawk clothing nearly none among us could or should attempt to wea·

No matter. The marketers ever more relentlessly ratchet up
perfection standard, extolling wildly unrealistic virtues of bea·
Each day, the chasm between reality and fantasy grows. As we g·
pudgier, the models in the display cases grow slinkier. At this rate,·
just a matter of time before the malnourished mannequins se·
control and begin sucking the nutrients out of us, which might·
be such a bad thing.

As I sat taking in the crazed mall scene, I decided we should all w·
on one collective New Year's resolution. All of us should vow to eat be·
and exercise more, to curb the empty calories and get up off the co·
and actually live a little.

While we're doing that, for better health and longer lives, we shoulc
let our daughters know that they don't need to be cartoonish toothp·
to be valued in our thin-obsessed culture.

No offense, Vicki, but you could really stand to put on a few poun·

⌒ *December 9, 2(*

When Music Died, Words Were Born

Do you remember what you were doing when John Lennon was sho·
don't, but I do remember, with a searing clarity, the moment 25 years ·
this morning when I belatedly heard the news.

I was a year out of college and working as a copy editor at a lacklu·
little newspaper in western Michigan. Because the paper was publishec
the afternoon, my shift began at an ungodly 4:45 a.m. My job was

n up the copy of others—the best I could often hope for was to
lge the truly awful up to merely mediocre—and then put a headline
it.

On December 8, 1980, I went to bed early without turning on the
vision or radio, clueless about the seismic shock waves emanating from
west side of Central Park in New York. The next morning I walked
o the newsroom unaware, and the other copy editors—older men who
eled in pushing my buttons—gleefully awaited me, Associated Press
y in hand.

"Your little hero Johnny Lennon bit the big one last night," one of
m, a washed-up back-bencher named Brandon, said.

literally reeled backward. I stuttered and stumbled. "He what?" I
ed, trying to process it. They all found this immensely amusing.

walked to the empty sports department and called my older brother
New York, waking him. "Did you hear?" I asked.

No Words Needed

had, the night before as he walked home from work through
ntral Park, and he had joined thousands of others in the im-
•mptu vigil outside the former Beatle's apartment building. We just
there on the phone, not saying much, not needing to.

Other icons of our age had "bit the big one," as Brandon would say—
is, Jimi, Janis, Morrison—and yet this was different.

The others had died of their own excesses. Lennon, publicly and
nfully, had worked through his, finding peace in the simple joys of
nerhood. And he was killed by one of us, a deranged fan carrying a
py of J. D. Salinger's *The Catcher in the Rye*.

If the Beatles provided the soundtrack for my youth, J. D. Salinger
vided the written text. Holden Caulfield—crazy, pitiable, confused,
predictable Holden—was a little bit of all of us from that time, just as
s Lennon, struggling to find his way, wearing his anguish on his sleeve.

And these two towering cultural icons came crashing together

outside the Dakota apartments in a way that no one anticipated. Inst
karma's gonna get you. . . . And yet, not like this.

The fact that his death came just one day after the anniversary
another generation's cultural earthquake—Pearl Harbor—only
tensified the feeling that this was something far more than jus
celebrity murder.

Inside Treatment

Back at the copy desk, the news chief, a World War II veteran who
19-year-old had dropped bombs on Berlin, had relegated Lennon's de
to two paragraphs on an inside page.

"You're kidding," I said.

Two hours later, the paper's editor, a no-nonsense veteran who
survived the bombing of Pearl Harbor, arrived. He glanced over the ne
budget, stopping at the Lennon story, slated for the "In Brief" roundu

He looked at me, and for the first time sought my opinion. "Thi
big, isn't it?" he asked.

"It's really big," I told him.

He seemed to grasp what my coworkers could not: that, like P
Harbor, this event was about to shut the door forever on a generatic
blissful naïveté and innocence.

All you need is love. . . . Right.

We ripped up the front page that morning and stripped
Lennon story across the top. Then my editor, this relic from a simp
time when good and evil were more clearly defined, turned to
and asked if I would write a first-person commentary on h
Lennon's death affected me.

It was the first column of my life, and when I had completed it, I kn
this was what I was meant to do.

In the crazy snowball of unanticipated circumstance that is life, f
shots on a New York City sidewalk reverberated outward, touching m
of us in unique ways.

or me that day, something inside died. And something was born.

⌒⌒⌒⌒⌒⌒○ January 6, 2006

You've Got Spam
AOL's Trial CDs

I hauled the fifth bulging bag of trash to the curb after the holidays, I
w I had finally had enough.

The packaging that comes with nearly every purchase in this
ntry, be it fast food or appliances or underwear, was totally out of
d. Do we really need that pint-size action figure double-boxed
shrink-wrapped and bound to a cardboard slab with nylon straps?
we worried he'll escape?

Do we think those zucchini will somehow taste better sold on a foam
and wrapped in enough cellophane to cover the Wachovia Center?

had recycled as much paper and plastic as I could, and still my family of
was contributing mounds to the landfill—most of it useless packaging
came into our house with gifts and immediately went into the trash. It
obscene.

That's when I spotted the enemy. In the top of an open trash can,
ting to join the parade of flotsam on the curb, sat two unopened,
tic-wrapped boxes that had appeared in my mailbox days earlier like
nany uninvited packages before them.

f an old flame were mailing me unwanted items, I'd be filing a stalker
nplaint with the local police. But these weren't from an old flame.

They were from America Online.

One was addressed to me by name, the other to "Current Resident."
ch contained identical materials: shiny new CDs and an offer to "Try
L 90 days risk-free!"

An Uninvited Guest

The only problem was I didn't want to try AOL, risk-free or not. I'd b
there, done that, and moved on to another Internet service provider y
earlier. And yet, with the regularity of rainfall, the unwanted CDs sho
ered in. As soon as they would arrive, I would drop them in the trash.

Maybe it was the postholiday grumpies, but I said out loud, "Not
time." I pulled the two AOL boxes out of the trash and scrawled in b
letters across them: "Refused! Return to sender." Man, it felt good.

The next morning, before dropping them in the mail, I decidec
check with the post office. I explained I was fed up by these unsolici
mailings.

"It's trash," the clerk said. "Throw it away."

"But I don't want to throw them away," I said. I tried to tell her ab
the landfills and the packaging and the bags of trash, but she cut me o

"We will not deliver it, sir."

I called a second post office and got the same answer. The bulk-
postage used by AOL and other mass mailers does not include ret
service. "Unfortunately, you'll have to get rid of them yourself,"
clerk said.

I scoured the AOL Web site, thinking it must have information on h
to return these unwanted disks at the company's expense. I clicked
"Discover All Things AOL" and discovered everything except how to g
the cursed things back. I clicked on "spam" (after all, wasn't that what
was?), but again no luck.

Headed for the Trash

In my Internet searching, I discovered a group (www.nomoreaolcds.cc
dedicated to ending the wasteful practice of sending out millions
unsolicited CDs, many of which will end up in the trash. The Califorr
based group is collecting unwanted AOL CDs, and when it
gathered one million, it plans to truck them to the company's headquar
in Virginia and dump them on the front steps. I want to be there for th

contemplated mailing the CDs back to AOL (22000 AOL Way,
lles, VA 20166). But why should I pay to return something I never
ed for?

Finally, I found a toll-free number (1-800-466-5463) and quickly got
ough to a helpful AOL sales rep named Mike, who was eager to sign me
When I told him I just wanted to be removed from the mailing list, he
l, "Hold, please."

Of course, I was disconnected.

On my second call, after navigating a maze of automated prompts, I reached
olite man named Mbuso in South Africa. I never knew Pennsylvania could
pronounced so many ways. Mbuso took my information and promised
t my days of receiving these ecological obscenities were behind me.

That still doesn't solve the problem of the two double-disk boxed sets
ttering my desk. Who knows, maybe I'll take up target shooting.

February 17, 2006

With This Ring, Show Some Class

right, men. We need to talk.

About The Ring.

Yes, that ring. The one Mario Mele, a former Montgomery County
missioner, gave to his then-sweetheart, Janet Grace, last spring.

The ring that made a very big statement about love and devotion and
ong commitment. A statement to the tune of two and one-third carats
$35,000.

The ring that Mele several weeks later wanted back after he decided
., you know what? Maybe marriage wasn't the best idea after all.

That ring.

Women, feel free to jump in here, but this really is a discussion we
n need to have. And the question is this: Guys, when you give a girl

a ring and then decide you've made a big mistake, what's the ri
course?

Not the legal course or the financially savvy course. The right cour
The honorable course.

As the whole nation now seems to know, the spurned bride-to
did not return the mammoth mineral. Instead, she sold the prince
cut diamond, gave the money to charity, and kept the setting as a
minder, one guesses, of the hard knocks that can accompany even
biggest rocks.

Mele, 64, sued his 46-year-old ex-fiancée, demanding the full value
the ring, plus $100,000 for his trouble.

She dug in her heels. Ah, fickle love, from gauzy romance to emb
rassingly public fights over the division of property before the first fis
of rice ever had a chance to fly.

A Gentleman's Choice

The lawsuit was surging forward until this week, when national media
tention suddenly put the fickle suitor and his jilted bride-to-be in
spotlight. She came off looking sympathetic; he came off looking, well

A guy proposes and less than two months later un-proposes? He g
an extravagantly expensive piece of jewelry—and then asks for it back

No man likes to look wishy-washy, and no man likes to look che
Mele was looking a lot like both.

With the national spotlight on them, the former lovebirds qui
resolved the lawsuit this week. And they both lived happily ever
Oops, wait. Wrong ending.

And they both agreed not to disclose terms of the agreement. Th
we go.

We know what Pennsylvania case law says—that an engagement rin
considered a "conditional gift" that still belongs to the suitor until
moment the deal is sealed with a kiss on the wedding altar, at which ti
it becomes the property of the bride.

But what does the human heart say? Come on, men, help me out here.
hen you give a woman a ring, what's your intention? Are you really
ving it to her, or just allowing her to hold your property on her finger
til she coughs up her end of the bargain?

It's more than that? Or at least isn't it supposed to be?

Rules of Engagement

I were making the rules, they would come down to this: A gift is
gift, and givers don't take back what they have bestowed. Men,
hen you give a ring, the ring is hers.

Women, if you change your mind and dump your suitor in the dust
fore ever getting to the whole "till death do we part" part, at least have
e decency to return the ring, even though you don't have to.

Men, if you are the ones doing the dumping, say goodbye not only to
e no-longer Miss Right but also to the large chunk of your savings that
lped your local jeweler send his children to really good colleges.

In the bigger scheme, the ring is chump change. Even a $35,000 ring.

Here's the moral of the story:

If you need to ask for the return of your ring, you spent too much
r it.

If you need to wonder if she's worth it, she's not.

If you wake up one day after proposing with a pit in your stomach, and
u know—just know—that it's all wrong, that this is not the person you
nt to spend the rest of your life with, listen to your gut and be thankful
u're figuring it out now, not on your honeymoon.

If you're a gentleman, you will let her down as gently as you know
w.

You'll blame yourself.

You won't mention the ring.

You will know you're getting off cheaply, even without getting it back.

A Helping Hand, a Helping of Grace

After December's tsunami claimed countless thousands of lives and l
millions more homeless, many Americans opened their checkbooks.

The Rev. Stanley Hagberg packed a sleeping bag, kissed his w
goodbye, and caught a flight into the heart of darkness.

For two months, Hagberg, a Conservative Baptist minister fro
Hatboro, slogged through muck and debris on the Indonesian island
Sumatra, helping in any way he could.

He carried sacks of rice, delivered cooking oil, shoveled mud o
of homes, painted flood-stained classrooms. Mostly, he listened
grief-stricken villagers who had lost everything—their homes, the
livelihoods, their children—bared their souls. "Everyone had a sto
to tell," said Hagberg, 66, who arrived back in Philadelphia l
month.

The territory of Aceh on the northern tip of Sumatra, where
arrived February 7, was the closest landfall to the earthquake th
spawned the tsunami that struck on December 26. A wall of wa
estimated at 100 feet tall slammed the western coastline, wiping o
everything in its path. The official casualty count was 126,000 dead a
40,000 missing, but Hagberg said locals believe the numbers to be
higher.

"As far as the eye could see in all directions, it was just nothing but le
eled foundations," he said last week from his office at the Norman
Farms Estates retirement community in Blue Bell, where he is chaplain

A Higher Calling

When the call had come asking him to join a Baptist relief mission to t
devastated area, Hagberg hesitated.

He was no stranger to the country, having spent 16 years with his wife, ancy, as Baptist missionaries in Indonesian Borneo.

But that was nearly a quarter-century ago. He wondered if he was ill up to the rigors of such a job. "I was thinking of all the reasons I ouldn't go, but I realized it was just something God wanted me to ɔ," he said.

Today, the minister believes the experience changed his life.

From the depths of one of the worst natural disasters in recorded story, he found a bright, shining light. It was the light of a shared umanity that transcended cultural and religious differences.

Aceh, the territory where he volunteered, is a stronghold of fundamen-list Islam. It is also a hotbed of a long-running rebel insurgency against e Indonesian government. Before the tsunami hit, Aceh was largely a osed society, suspicious of outsiders.

Enter the bespectacled and soft-spoken Hagberg, who kept his hristian beliefs to himself, knowing he was there to help, not proselytize.

A Conservative Baptist minister thrown together with fundamentalist luslims in a ravaged and chaotic land? You might think this would be a cipe for a whole new level of seismic upheaval. But as Hagberg slogged rough the mosquito-infested heat and humidity, he found just the ɔposite—something beyond beautiful, approaching the sublime.

New Friendships

e came expecting suspicion; he left having found that most elusive state ˉ grace—brotherhood blind to race, creed, or nationality.

"They were just very kind, loving, and affectionate," Hagberg said of e people whose lives he touched and who touched his. They were ɔofoundly grateful to know an American traveled so far for no reason her than to hold out a helping hand.

"You really become part of each others' lives in that situation," he flected. "Talk about feeling a person's pain. You want to weep with em for their loss, you really do."

One man told him, "You are a member of my family. You are n
brother."

A local leader, overwhelmed with gratitude, offered to build a hou
for Hagberg so he could return with his wife to live in the man's villag
"That, I think, is the greatest compliment I've ever been given," Hagbe
said.

He took some lessons home with him. He knows now that action
speak louder than words, and that empathy is a gift returned many tim
over. He learned that in matters of life and death, differences melt away.

Through the jungle of despair, he glimpsed an elusive path—the or
that leads to peace on Earth.

August 7, 200

Summer and Smoke

The year was 1967, and in the Summer of Love, as it would becom
known, the world seemed to be pulling apart from all directions.

Two of my cousins were fighting in Vietnam; the others we
protesting the war in Ann Arbor. My older brother was growing h
hair long; my mother was saying extra rosaries that she wouldn't lo
him entirely.

Jimi Hendrix, Janis Joplin, and The Who stormed the country
Monterey, and the Beatles released *Sgt. Pepper's Lonely Hearts Cl*
Band, an album that filled our home all summer from the stereophon
record player with the flip-up turntable.

In my little world, it was the summer my best friend, John Rosser, an
I set off to buy our first pack of cigarettes.

We were 10 years old.

As memory serves me, it was more Rosser's idea than mine, but I was
willing co-conspirator.

Many of the older kids in our neighborhood, which was nestle

inst a lake outside Detroit, were smoking. The young teens with their
-karts made with lawn-mower engines; the older teens with their
uped-up Camaros and GTOs; the high-school girls we could only
eam about, all blonde and bronzed, who worshiped the sun down at the
ighborhood beach.

They smoked and looked beautiful. We wanted to, as well. So on a hazy
t morning we set off on our matching Schwinn Typhoon bicycles for
e Sylvan Lanes Bowling Alley, several miles from our homes and well
yond the bounds of parental permission. Between us we had 35 cents—
e exact price of one pack of cigarettes.

We chose the bowling alley because it had a vending machine in an
ter foyer. We chose morning because we knew the place would be
ipty.

We were quaking with fear.

I played lookout, waiting with the bikes while Rosser went in. He
urned seconds later to report he had gotten one dime in the ma-
ine before hearing a noise and fleeing.

It was my turn. I strolled in as nonchalantly as I could, my knees
ocking, and pushed the quarter into the slot—then sprinted out as
ough a rottweiler were fast on my heels.

We stood together in the parking lot summoning our nerve. All
at was left to do was select our brand—it had to be Marlboro; all the
ol kids smoked Marlboro—and pull the knob. This time we went in
gether.

"You pull, I'll grab," Rosser said.

I spotted the Marlboro placard and pulled. The wrong knob.

Out came a pack of True cigarettes. Rosser could not have looked
ore horror-stricken had a rotting rat fallen from the machine. Oh no,
I cigarettes!

There was no time to lament. We could see adults inside.

"Let's go!" Rosser yelled, cramming the pack of Trues down the crotch
his shorts. We hopped on our bikes and pedaled off full speed, not stop-

ping until we reached the vacant waterfront lot across from my hou
There was nothing on it except a rickety stairway leading down a ste
wooded slope to the lake.

Near the water's edge was an oak tree with a hollow in its trunk—c
stash spot for all sorts of juvenile contraband over the years. It was th
we peeled off the cellophane, tugged open the foil wrapper and ea
placed one of the slim cigarettes between our lips.

Rosser struck the match, and we lit up. We must have looked ridic
lous, puffing and coughing, our eyes watering, our heads spinning, o
stomachs churning.

For being cool, smoking sure wasn't much fun. Nonetheless, v
finished our cigarettes, then lit a third, passing it between us.

For good measure as we smoked, Rosser and I shouted eve
curse word we could think of into the treetops. Just for the thrill
it. Just to spite the Catholic nuns who taught us at Our Lady
Refuge up the street. We wanted them to know they hadn't won t
indoctrination war yet.

How grown up it seemed, smoking and swearing in the very sar
breath. (Neither of us would go on to smoke as adults, though v
both occasionally still swear at the treetops.)

Rosser and I buried the butts and stashed the cigarette pack in t
tree hollow, then headed to my house, where we crept past my moth
at the kitchen sink and locked ourselves in the bathroom to sw
toothpaste in our mouths. We felt like soldiers after battle. With blus
and bravado, we laughed and jabbed each other at the sink.

We were 10 with no cares or worries in this troubled, confusing wor
We were romping through the dog days of summer at full, blissful gallc
We had just conquered our first cigarette, as awful as it was.

It only made sense to celebrate by giving *Sgt. Pepper* another wh
before heading to the beach where the pretty girls with the burnish
skin waited to ignore us once again.

One Violent Summer, Two Worlds Collided

y uncle is an old man now, a retired priest who lives in a log cabin in
e country and spends his days growing vegetables to give away.

But in the summer of 1967, he was the pastor of St. Catherine's
tholic Church, an inner-city parish in Detroit that was 40 minutes and
world away from the lakefront suburban neighborhood where I was
owing up.

To his parishioners, he was Monsignor Vincent Howard. To his nieces
d nephews he was simply Father Vin, an irrepressible practical joker
o would greet you with a slap on the back—and drop an ice cube
wn your shirt. Or tell you to look out the window, then gleefully steal
e cherry off your sundae.

On July 23 of that year, a Sunday night, my uncle was not joking. He
s scared for his life.

Without warning, a large swath of Detroit had exploded in what
uld become one of the country's most violent race riots, a five-day
nflagration that would claim 43 lives and entire blocks of the city.
res were burning, firefighters were taking gunfire, the police were
ned down in their precinct houses—and my uncle was trying to
tect his flock.

"The riot was going on all around us. That night I had 35 people
ying in the rectory," he told me recently. "They slept on the steps and
the floors. We couldn't raise our heads above the windowsills; we had
crawl because we were afraid we would get shot."

He was particularly worried about two families with young children
ose homes were close to the violence. Early the next morning, he
ked up the telephone.

"I called your mother and she welcomed them out there," he recalled.

That is where my memory begins.

I remember that morning, watching Detroit burn live on the tele-
sion, and Father Vin's Chevrolet pulling into our driveway, loaded w
children. Seven of them poured out, each holding a paper grocery sack
clothes.

As I recall, the youngest was about 8 and the oldest 15, a mix of b
and girls from two families.

Until that day, my world was my quiet neighborhood. It was sw
lessons and horseback riding, Little League and touch football. I was
and had only the vaguest notion that places like Detroit, with th
poverty and festering racial tensions, existed.

These kids, scared and visibly impoverished, were just as shocked
my world as I was by theirs. We considered ourselves middle class—c
car, one black-and-white television—but I could tell they saw us as i
possibly rich. We had a modern house on a park-like lot, and, down t
street, a neighborhood beach and a dock with a sailboat tied to it.

In my suburban world, I had always thought I was pretty tough
wasn't tough. These kids were tough. I was instantly intimidated. We e
each other with awkwardness and suspicion.

My mother ordered everyone into bathing suits and down to t
beach. Her purpose, I later would learn, was to have the opportunity
wash their clothes.

Only when we reached the water's edge did I realize that not all k
grow up with such a privilege. They stared nervously at the water
which I was so at ease. Not one of them knew how to swim.

The children stayed with us for five days while the riots raged
the beat of the Lovin' Spoonful's "Summer in the City" on the rad
The girls took over the bedroom and the boys slept in our tent-trai
in the backyard. My mom, her mother-hen instinct in overdri
whipped up huge batches of hot-dog casserole and baked beans, a
ordered her new adoptees, just like her own kids, to get in the t

d not come out until their feet were clean. At night, we roasted arshmallows and stared up at the stars, invisible to them in the city.

Gradually, we became friends. We rode bikes through the neigh-orhood together, ran through the woods and splashed in the water. taught the boy closest to my age how to dog paddle, and he taught e how draw comic-book characters.

Day by day, hour by hour, we were figuring out that, for all our fferences of place and privilege, we were not all that different.

In the end, we were all just kids. Kids who loved ice cream and hated ths. Kids who liked bare feet and dreaded the return to school. Kids ho hid from chores and found mischief.

Through violent upheaval, our paths had crossed. Serendipitously, our parate worlds had come together, not with a crash but with a gasp of utual awe.

For them, I imagine my life was a fairly tale, a tantalizing dream from hich they soon enough would awaken. They had been plucked from eir burning block and deposited here where all was safe and clean and ell. They stayed just long enough to taste what lay beyond their grasp.

The greater lesson was mine to take. These children were my wake-up ll. Never again could I so blithely take for granted all my parents had orked to provide. No longer could I presume that children grow up ual or that life is an even playing field.

On that last day, when it came time to say goodbye, we hugged and omised to write. Then they piled into Father Vin's Chevrolet and aded back to the smoldering ashes of their neighborhood. Their happy, eaming faces smiled back at me as they disappeared into the distance.

Talkin' 'Bout the Generations

The first time I saw The Who, I was a high school senior, and my lastir memory of that day was the terrifying sensation that I was about to I crushed.

It was December 1975 at the Silverdome in Pontiac, Michigan, cavernous venue that was then home to the Detroit Lions. Tens thousands of fans surrounded the place, waiting for the doors to ope General admission.

My best friend, Ray, and I had arrived early and were near the fror The crowd began to surge forward even though the gates remaine locked. Tighter and tighter we were squeezed until I could not mov my arms and could barely breathe. And then we were squeezed eve tighter.

Just as panic began to sweep the crowd, the gates swung open ar we poured forward, like flotsam in a raging river. It was a fitting sta for a night of volatile, reckless rock-and-roll—music like I had nev experienced before. Visceral, raging, ear-piercing, all cloaked in a ha of marijuana smoke.

The second time I saw The Who—the two surviving members, th is—was last week at the Wachovia Center. My, how we've all change these last 31 years.

As my colleague Dan DeLuca noted in his review, the packed hou was dominated by middle-age parents with their teenage childre Fathers and sons in matching Who T-shirts. Moms and daughte singing together, ". . . we won't get fooled again."

A Family Affair

here were plenty of young adults in attendance, too—a testament to the
tergenerational pull of this iconic rock band—but all around me the
thering had more the feel of soccer camp than a reunion of arguably
e wildest bad boys of rock.

I did not detect a single whiff of marijuana.

My wife and I had brought our three children, ages 14, 12, and 9, Who
ns all, to experience this cultural phenomenon before it was too late.

And by the end of the night, I acutely felt the push of time.

Pete Townshend, still hard-rocking, was grizzled. Roger Daltrey, that
hereal, blue-eyed pretty boy every high school girl once craved, was
oticeably slower, his vocal range diminished, his microphone gym-
astics a shadow of his earlier days. During one song, he missed his
ue and apologized, "I can't hear the beat." Later he complained about
ing half-deaf.

It was like watching a pair of proud lions, the once unchallenged
ngs of their jungle, fighting back against their inevitable decline.
hey could still rock, no doubt about it, but there was a poignancy in
eir performance, an unspoken acknowledgement that their days of
ling arenas and blasting out power chords were numbered.

In the men's room, a fan who appeared to be in his 50s said to my
-year-old, "Remember this night, kid. The night you saw Pete
ownshend and Roger Daltrey together onstage." He knew what I
ew: that the sun was setting on yet another icon of the '60s rock
volution.

Passing the Baton

they were not the same rock stars, I was no longer the same fan. I
alized that as I watched drummer Zak Starkey, son of Beatles
ummer Ringo Starr, come amazingly close to capturing the frenetic
ajesty of The Who's original drummer, Keith Moon. I felt a swell of

emotion in my chest. A father's emotion. I leaned over to my w
and said, "His dad must be so proud." And I meant it.

This was a rock concert, and I knew I should be, well, rocking. Bu
found myself glancing at my own children, their heads nodding to t
music, and wondering where life's magical mystery tour might take the
Surely somewhere I could not even imagine.

The baton was passing from one generation to the next, from the lio
to the cubs, from fathers to sons. The future was theirs now.

After the last song, the crowd gave the aging rockers the standing ov
tion they deserved, perhaps as much for what they were, what they w
always be in our collective memory, as for what they are now.

Then Townshend darted off the stage with adolescent agility while l
cohort hobbled off gingerly on what appeared to be arthritic knees.

As another graying rocker put it, rock-and-roll will never die. But
practitioners—those once eternally young gods of the stage—will inde
fade away.

October 9, 20

Dogged Writers in the Big House

So I'm at the White House having breakfast with the First Lady . . .

I know, it sounds like the opening line of a bad joke. But there I am
a recent Saturday, noshing on salmon and French toast beneath a gi
portrait of Benjamin Franklin.

The closest I've ever been to power was in 1968 when I held the f
for the governor of Michigan. I'm pretty easily starstruck.

"Is this really happening?" I whispered to my wife.

She opened her blazer to show me the embossed paper ha
towel she'd snatched from the powder room. "It's really happenin
she answered.

I glanced at the marine guards in their dress uniforms and wondered
at federal laws we were breaking.

Yes, we. I reached into my pocket and showed Jenny that I, too, had
loined a souvenir—a cocktail napkin stamped with the words: "Seal of
President of the United States."

"Guantanamo, here we come," I said.

For the record, Jenny and I weren't the only ones nabbing souvenirs.
e word was out among the 150 or so breakfast guests that the presi-
ntial paper products were the hottest ticket in town.

We were all there for one simple reason: Many of us had written
oks. And Laura Bush, that former librarian, loves books.

She loves them so much that six years ago she launched the National
ok Festival with the Library of Congress to bring authors and readers
gether to celebrate the written word.

Each year the festival has grown. And on that Saturday, 100,000 readers
all ages poured onto the National Mall to attend book readings and
nings. If you fear the written word is on the verge of extinction, and
t electronic gadgetry has eclipsed old-fashioned words on paper, the
ne on the Mall would brighten your outlook.

The crowd included every imaginable demographic slice. But it
s the young people who caught my eye. School children collecting
tographs, high schoolers with pierced eyebrows, college students
ing notes. One student told me she drove all the way from
nherst, Massachusetts.

The written word was boldly alive on the Mall that day, as big and
zenly virile as the Washington Monument itself.

But before the festival came the breakfast, and before the breakfast—the
vious night—came a black-tie gala at the Library of Congress for the
hors and sponsors, attended by President and Mrs. Bush, Secretary of
te Condoleezza Rice and other administration officials.

"Hey," I said, spotting Attorney General Alberto Gonzales, at the n
table. "It's the torture guy!"

But we weren't there to debate torture or unconstitutional detainme
or the ever-bleaker quagmire in Iraq. We were here to agree on one thi
the value of words on paper.

The invited authors, poets, and illustrators covered the spectru
Legal thriller writers Scott Turow and (Philly's own) Lisa Scottoline w
on the program. So were investigative reporter Bob Woodward a
Khaled Hosseini, author of the acclaimed *The Kite Runner*, as w
Pulitzer Prize winners Doris Kearns Goodwin, Taylor Branch, a
Geraldine Brooks.

Yeah, and bringing up the rear, me—that columnist who wrote ab
life with an insane Labrador retriever.

All invited by Mrs. Bush to send the message that books matter.

She thanked the writers "for the many solitary hours you spe
working to enlighten and inform and inspire and entertain all
rest of us." When I had a few moments with her, I thanked her
championing something that matters.

In the English language, it all comes down to this: Twenty-six lett
when combined correctly, can create magic. Twenty-six letters form
foundation of a free, informed society.

Whatever you think of the president and his administration—a
frankly I don't think much of them—let's give credit where credit is d

Laura Bush is doing more to promote reading and literacy than
First Lady before her, and perhaps more than anyone in the coun
today. She is using her substantial bully pulpit to spotlight reading a
literacy and to hook children—the next generation—as lifetime lov
of books.

The president's legacy might be in question; his wife's is secure.

Well done, Mrs. Bush.

And thanks for the cool napkins.

A Searing Lesson in Forgiveness

hindsight, I realize I was driving too fast, especially given the
n-slicked roads.

Ahead of me at an intersection, a car was stopped with its left blinker
. I bore down, expecting it to turn out of my path at any second.

But the car did not turn. By the time I hit the brakes it was too late. I
dded and slammed into its rear end, catapulting it into cross traffic.

Miraculously, the other vehicles all avoided the car, but I realized
tantly my moment of poor judgment could easily have resulted in
: death of an innocent stranger.

Across the intersection, we both pulled into a parking lot. The man in-
e looked like he could have been a bar bouncer, large and intimidating.

He wasn't hurt and neither was I. His car did not even have a dent
ere I hit it.

"Man, you almost got me creamed," the driver said.

I apologized profusely. He had every right to be angry, and I was braced
 him to get in my face, poke a finger in my chest and dress me down
th a string of obscenities. People had been beaten up, even shot, over
ser transgressions.

Then he did an amazing thing. The stranger shook my hand and said,
 was an accident. Don't worry about it."

The F Word

at was years ago, but the moment has stuck with me because it put
: on the receiving end of an important lesson. I had erred and he had
given.

Forgiveness.

We all want to think we are capable of it. And for most of us, most the time, we are.

We can forgive a child who disobeys. Or a delivery driver w accidentally knocks over our mailbox. Perhaps even a thief who ta what is ours.

But what about an offense far worse? Unspeakably, unimagina worse?

What about a stranger who barges into a country schoolhouse, lines 10 innocent children against the chalkboard—and opens fire?

What parent, what community, could forgive that?

We now know the answer.

Within hours of Charles Carl Roberts IV's murderous assault on Amish school in Lancaster County on October 2, the local Am community was already expressing forgiveness.

Even before they had a chance to bury their dead daughters. Even they huddled bedside as other victims clung to life by the most tenuous threads. Complete and total forgiveness.

What was done was done, and the killer, too, was now dead. amount of anger or vengeance-seeking would bring the children ba or the killer to justice. The Amish had two choices: Descend the d staircase into bitterness, or follow the tenets of their faith and rise abc it. They believe all acts, even one as monstrous as this, are part of th God's inexplicable plan.

And so they forgave.

Mercy Amid Grief

Amish neighbors went to the killer's home to console his wife and ot relatives. They attended his funeral and invited his widow to attend at le one of the murdered girl's funerals. As thousands of dollars poured in fr around the world to help the families of the victims, the Amish set u fund for the killer's own children.

Unbelievable.

Unbelievable and somehow beautiful all at once.

It is the stuff sermons are built around. If the Amish can forgive such a
ustly violation, can't we all try to be just a little more forgiving of the
hts and hurts and wrongs of daily life?

The simple people know what many of us still have not figured out,
t the ever-escalating violence of vengeance has no end, and that the
l of revenge etches the human heart with deep and permanent scars.

Imagine if the ethic of unilateral forgiveness could envelop the Sunnis
l Shiites in Iraq, the Catholics and Protestants in Ireland, the Jews and
estinians in Israel. Imagine if it could permeate the streets of America,
ere rival gangs kill over colors and young men settle scores over respect
h 9mm Glocks.

The Amish have found the road to a higher place. The rest of us could
worse than to be a little more like them.

November 3, 2006

Flying's Fearful New Annoyances

ays something about my state of mind that I found myself on a
ht from Pennsylvania to Texas last week counting the contents of
in-flight snack.

dumped the bag onto the tray table and used the eraser end of a
icil to line up the contents in little rows.

My "premium blend" power snack consisted of exactly nine and a half
nuts, five and a quarter sesame sticks, and five lonely mini-pretzels.
gether, this gastronomic feast totaled a whopping one-half ounce.
Bon appetit, passengers!

isn't it nice to know the airlines are doing their part to address the
ional obesity epidemic? I'm just grateful they didn't stick me with
"dieters' blend."

I don't normally spend my time obsessing over snack mixes, but
is what the sorry state of air travel in America has done to me. Tur
me into a raving soybean counter.

Remember the good old days when fliers loved to hate the airline fo
Back in those days of yore when there actually was airline food? Y
know. I'm giving away my age.

Shoes Off, Please

The food is just a small part of it.

The joys of modern air travel now begin at the security check-in
where we line up like cattle, removing shoes and blazers, whipping
belts, clutching trousers to keep them from heading south.

No one wants to grumble about measures to keep the nation safe fi
terrorism, so we shuffle silently through in our stocking feet. But hone
some of the security rules are plain dumb.

Somehow I don't feel any safer knowing that the grandma in fron
me in line just had to throw out her four-ounce bottle of Oil of Olay

Immediately after the liquid-explosive scare several weeks a
anything liquid or gel had to go. Thousands of dollars worth
cosmetics and soft drinks were tossed out. The terrorists, I'm su
were mightily amused.

Then the Transportation Security Administration tweaked the rule
allow travelers to carry whatever liquids and gels they could fit int
one-quart plastic bag, as long as no one item was more than three oun

I was in the security line a couple of weeks ago and the man in fron
me had his toiletry kit boiled down to the bare essentials—tiny travel s
of toothpaste, deodorant, and mouthwash. But he forgot the plastic ba

The TSA inspector told him, no baggie, no go. The man dumped th
in the trash. And for what?

When my turn came, I had my essentials in the baggie, having lear
my lesson on a previous flight when all my liquids were confiscated.

But one of my items was a six-ounce toothpaste tube. "This container
o large," the TSA inspector said.

But it's nearly empty," I told him. At best, it had an ounce left in it.

Doesn't matter," he said. "We go by the container size, not the
ents."

Some Common Sense

anted to retort: "So it's OK to have six ounces of toothpaste in two
e-ounce containers, but not one ounce in a six-ounce container?"

knew where arguing would get me. "Whatever," I said and tossed it.

We need security, I realize that. We need rules. But a little common
e would be nice, too.

The overzealous security rules wouldn't be so bad if checking luggage
not such a crap shoot.

My son and I flew from Philadelphia to California for a long
ekend a few months ago, and I did something I never do—
cked our luggage. Big mistake. The bags didn't show up until we
e nearly ready to return home.

Even when bags are not lost, the waits to retrieve them in baggage
m can exceed the flight time. Especially here in Philadelphia, home to
why-hurry-I'm-hourly school of customer service.

J.S. Airways' baggage delays and losses in Philadelphia have become
mbarrassing, the airline's top brass went public with a plan to fix the
blem. I'll believe it when I see it.

or the beleaguered passenger, the choices are bleak: Check your bag
pray you'll someday see it again, or carry it through security and face
toothpaste gestapo.

The only consolation is knowing, once you finally make your flight, a
ty half-ounce snack awaits you.

ust try not to spoil your appetite.

Mortality Check Is in the Mail

The letter arrived unannounced at my home, hidden amid junk ma

It came in a plain envelope with a simple street address on the back. T
was no outward hint as to its contents, and for good reason. I would l
promptly thrown it away.

Yes, it was that letter. The one no one wants to receive but all one
will. The letter that makes an IRS audit seem like a lottery prize.

The one that slaps you hard on the face and tells you once and fc
that you never again will fit into those 30-inch-waist jeans.

"Dear Mr. John J. Grogan," it began.

I scanned the opening paragraph, picking out the operative phr:
"fully eligible . . . membership . . . benefits . . . life over 50."

Life. Over 50.

I began to pray. Oh, Lord, please, no. Not that. Anything but that.

For whom does the American Association of Retired Persons trol
trolls for me.

My official AARP membership card, No. 1567627, was attached.

"Honey," I called to my wife. "Where's the bourbon?"

Counting the Days

For the record, I am not 50. Not even close. Fifty remains a faraway sp
on the horizon. I remain a proud member of the forty-something dec
Some of my best friends are thirty-somethings. A few are even fresh-fa
twenty-somethings.

I still do ridiculously foolhardy things like teeter from a high lac
holding a chain saw.

I am not 50, OK? That's still four months, 10 days, and 17 hours av
Not that anyone is counting.

But could the AARP wait?

The letter tried to lure me in with a long list of "benefits and services" ned at nascent geezers-in-waiting.

A safe-driving course, for starters. I couldn't help conjuring up a rrible premonition of me in a Buick Skylark tooling along at 43 h in the high-speed lane of Interstate 95. Nooooo!

My membership comes with a magazine to remind me that I'm on the wnhill slide to 100.

It offers regular updates on Social Security, an entitlement program I perfectly happy never to qualify for.

I also can use my AARP card, and I quote, "to save on shoes."

All colors, or just white?

I won't deny it. The arrival of my AARP card threw me into a total ık. This was my parents' organization. Why was it bugging me?

I tried to put the best spin on it. Finally, those bushy eyebrows I've vays craved would be coming into their own!

The Eternal Paterno

ıt there was no denying the harsh reality. Life's best chapters may still lie ead, but any way I spun it, the story line ended the same way.

At the cemetery.

That's when I thought about Joe Paterno. What better role model for e second half-century?

The Penn State coaching legend will turn 80 next month and still gets every morning to go to work.

Saturday he was flattened by two players who crashed into him, eaking his leg, but not his intensity.

I loved the photo of Paterno being carted off the field with his injured ʒ up. His face, equal parts disgust and impatience, said it all: Get the mn leg fixed so I can get back to work, will ya?

Not that I harbor fantasies of coaching college ball. But when I grow , I want to be like Jumpin' Joe Paterno.

Not a stubborn-as-a-mule coach. But someone who refuses to rel
to the ravages of time. Someone who embraces his passion witho
compromise and won't let go. Someone who tells age what it can
with itself.

A guy who won't slow down.

My father was a bit like Paterno that way. He hurled himself at life
bore every day, right up to his last. I would have put him, at 89, up agai
men 20 years younger.

An automotive engineer, he liked to say, "The worst possible thing
a car is to let it sit and idle." The same rule applies to the human machi

Bring it on, AARP. Bring on the membership cards and seni
discounts.

Fifty may be right around the corner. But as a great coach might
his players in the halftime pep talk of life: You're only as old as you
yourself be.

_____⌐ *November 24, 20*

Just Say No to Black Friday

Good morning, shoppers.

Today is the big day. The one that sends crazed bargain hunters into
salivating frenzy. The one that sends retailers and credit card compan
into a heroin-like state of bliss. The one that sends anyone still clinging
the real meaning of Christmas into the dumps.

Yes, today is the appropriately named Black Friday. A dark and gloo
and cynical day.

Around our region, tens of thousands of shoppers will work
yesterday's big turkey dinner by rising before dawn, jostling for parki
spaces, racing up and down aisles, lunging for the latest must-have to
and electronics, and waiting in long lines to pay.

Tempers will flare, heads will throb, feet will ache. But it will all

rth it because at the end of the day our cars will be filled with . . . stuff.
ff to show our loved ones how much we care.

You wouldn't think we famously materialistic Americans would
ed our own special day to ratchet the spending orgy up. But that's
lat today is.

Actually, that's not quite accurate. Today actually began yesterday. That
the Black Friday shopping kickoff actually got started at many stores on
anksgiving afternoon or evening.

Why spend the holiday at home with your family when you can get a
ad start on the purchases that mean so much more?

Finding Balance

hard, I know.

As parents, my wife and I struggle to find the right balance. In our
nds, we're giving our children a nice assortment of gifts without go-
g overboard. Then they compare notes with their friends, and I see
e disappointment on their faces. That Monopoly game instantly loses
luster when Tommy up the street whizzes by on his new all-terrain
ir-wheeler.

The new meaning of Christmas comes down to this: guilt. To avoid
we buy like there is no tomorrow. There's not much joy in it, but at
st we've covered.

Baby Jesus would be so proud.

May I make a modest proposal?

Just say no.

Say no to the rat race.

Say no to the hype.

Say no to the notion, carefully planted by marketers and advertisers,
at good parents who really care shower their children with obscene
lounts of toys and gifts—even if they need to max out their credit cards
do it.

Look away from the light, my friends. Block out the white no:
Ignore the "only X shopping days left" pitches.

The season is not about buying junior 26 different toys, most
which will be obsolete, broken, or ignored within weeks. It's not ab
spending on steroids. At least it didn't start out that way. You don't ne
to be particularly religious to recognize that.

Pricey Playthings

A teen in Allentown laid out $600 for the newly released and wil
hyped PlayStation 3—and minutes later was robbed of it at gunpoint.

I'm not sure which distresses me more: people robbing one anotl
with guns, or Sony shaking down kids for a $600 toy that, mark i
words, will be out-of-date in 24 months.

Last year, I wanted to give a special gift to a special friend who did a
for me in the previous months. I bought into the hype, thinking I neec
to spend several hundred dollars to convey the proper level of appreciatic
In the end, I spent zero.

Instead, I holed up in my basement night after night and slow
crafted a simple keepsake box out of a black walnut log that came fro
the woods behind my house. I sawed the log into planks, planed t
planks into boards, fitted the boards together, then sanded and varnish
and polished.

I'm no master craftsman, and the final product reflected that. But my frie
was touched by my efforts in a way no purchased gift could touch. The r
gift, though, was to me.

I rediscovered the true joy of gift giving. A joy unburdened by guilt
pressure or competition.

Here's the secret: It's about giving of yourself.

Today I plan to observe Black Friday by sitting home in front of t
fire with a good book. The mad march on the mall can be somebo
else's crusade. Care to join me?

An Army of One Takes on Litter

any given morning in Roxborough, you might spot a middle-aged
man bundled against the cold, making her way along Ridge Avenue,
ping to retrieve anything she finds in her path.

ou will know her because she will have a mixed-breed dog at her
, and, almost always, other people's discards in her hands.

he might stop to scoop up tossed fast food or a crumb-filled
ghnut bag or a beer can with one last swill inside.

If it's too disgusting I won't pick it up," she says. "If it's oozing or
ey, I won't touch it." Her name is Diane Bones, and she wants you
:now that she is not bag lady looking for her next meal. She is a
ıfully employed homeowner and proud resident of the neighbor-
d who is waging a one-woman battle against what she considers
·my No. 1: litter.

t's everywhere—blowing down the streets, covering the sidewalks and
 yards, Bones says.

When she moved into the city from Media, shortly after getting
ried in 2000, she noticed it immediately. And it drove her crazy.

I love living in the city," she says. "I love everything about it. My only
ıplaint is the litter."

Daily Good Deed

ł so Bones, 53, took it upon herself to pick up the messes left by
ngers. She has turned her morning power walk with Samantha, the
›herd mix, into a street-sprucing mission.

What does she snag on a typical walk?

 Soda cans, cigarette packs, candy wrappers, potato-chip bags,

newspapers, milk jugs, beer and booze bottles," she says. "On
street, litter is just an accepted way of life. People just walk right by

Bones lives across from an Acme, and she often picks up disca
packaging from items customers have just bought. Plastic bags from
nearby Rite-Aid blow about.

A couple of doors from her home sits Levering Elementary Sch
which Bones says is a source of a lot of the trash. Children drop
wrappers and soft-drink bottles without seeming to realize they're li
ing, she says.

Her route takes her near Roxborough High School. She has watc
students exit a nearby doughnut shop, dropping their trash as they wa

Sometimes she confronts them. "I will literally yell across R
Avenue, 'Pick that up!'" she says. Usually they do.

"They look startled. They don't think they're doing anything wron

The culprits are not just children. She has caught plenty of adul
the act, too, including a neighbor who blithely tossed a worthless lot
ticket out the window of her car.

"She didn't win, so we all lose," Bones grouses.

A Symbol of Surrender

What bugs her almost as much as the litterers are those who simply
over the trash, even if it is in their own yard or in front of their busin

She admits she's a bit obsessive about litter. She sees it as a cancer
eats away at civic pride and community fabric.

"Even through it seems like a minor problem, litter sets the t
for a we-don't-care attitude," Bones says. "It's symbolic of an apath
surrender. It's saying, 'You know what? I give up.'"

Bones is not about to give up.

When she moved in, there were no public trash cans near Lever
Elementary, and neighbors told her that was just the way it was.
made one call to then-Councilman Michael Nutter, and two tr
receptacles soon appeared outside the school.

One person's efforts really can make a difference.

Every morning, Bones picks up what she can, even as passersby stare, thinking she must be crazy or homeless or both. The next day, more trash always awaits her.

"Sometimes it does feel futile," she admits. "Some days, I ask why I even bother."

Still, she soldiers on.

"Have I made a difference? Who knows? I can't be responsible for the whole world, but I can be responsible for the little spot in front of my house.

"If my little corner of the world can look better, maybe it will start to snowball."